INTRODUCTION TO ART THERAPY
Faith in the Product

ABOUT THE AUTHOR

Bruce L. Moon is the Co-Director of the Clinical Internship in Art Therapy and the Director of the Clinical Art Therapy Graduate Intensive Summer Program at Harding Hospital, Worthington, Ohio. He is an art therapist, working primarily with the child and adolescent patients at Harding and he maintains a small private practice. He is an Adjunct Faculty Member of Lesley College. He has lectured and led workshops at many sites throughout the United States.

Bruce is an active painter and over-the-hill athlete. He and his wife Cathy and their two children, Jesse and Brea, live in a log home that they built together in the country outside Columbus, Ohio.

Author of two other texts, *Existential Art Therapy: The Canvas Mirror,* and *Essentials of Art Therapy Training and Practice,* he brings to the profession a rich tradition of training in art, education, theology and art therapy. The integration of these with his interests in existential philosophy, depth psychology, clinical work and training provides an engaging poetic and theoretical approach to the art therapy profession.

INTRODUCTION TO ART THERAPY

Faith in the Product

By

BRUCE L. MOON, M.A.C.E., M.Div., A.T.R.

With a Foreword by

Shaun McNiff, Ph.D.

And Contributions by

Robert Huestis, M.D.

John Reece, M.A.

CHARLES C THOMAS • PUBLISHER

Springfield • Illinois • U.S.A.

Published and Distributed Throughout the World by

CHARLES C THOMAS • PUBLISHER
2600 South First Street
Springfield, Illinois 62794-9265

© *1994 by* CHARLES C THOMAS • PUBLISHER
ISBN 0-398-05893-8 (cloth)
ISBN 0-398-06297-8 (paper)
Library of Congress Catalog Card Number: 93-36346

With THOMAS BOOKS *careful attention is given to all details of manufacturing
and design. It is the Publisher's desire to present books that are satisfactory as to their
physical qualities and artistic possibilities and appropriate for their particular use.*
THOMAS BOOKS *will be true to those laws of quality that assure a good name
and good will.*

Printed in the United States of America
SC-R-3

Library of Congress Cataloging-in-Publication Data

Moon, Bruce L.
    Introduction to art therapy : faith in the product / by Bruce L.
Moon : with a foreword by Shaun McNiff ; and contributions by Robert
Huestis, John Reece.
        p.   cm.
    Includes bibliographical references and index.
    ISBN 0-398-05893-8. — ISBN 0-398-06297-8 (pbk.)
    1. Art therapy. I. Huestis, Robert, 1945–   . II. Reece, John,
1955–   . III. Title.
    [DNLM: 1. Art Therapy. 2. Professional-Patient Relations.   WM
450.5.A8 M8181 1994]
RC489.A7M663 1994
616.89'1656 — dc20
DNLM/DLC
for Library of Congress   93-36346
                                                                                   CIP

FOREWORD

Introduction to Art Therapy offers Bruce Moon's most passionate and convincing call for the renewal of art therapy. The book is full of the inspiration and wisdom conveyed when a pioneer honestly describes his deepest personal instincts and those of art. More than any other book in the art therapy literature, this text fulfills Rudolf Arnheim's ideal of a psychology of art permeated by smells of the studio. All of my senses were aroused as I read Moon's descriptions of patients working with diverse materials—the sounds of a man chiseling concrete, cutting and bending tin, building stretchers and preparing canvas, squeezing wet clay. The clear and numerous vignettes show how art therapy is about action, constructing things, and making soul. I am intrigued by the subtitle, "Faith in the Product," because the book is so strongly focused on "trusting the process." But process and product are two sides of a coin, necessary partners in creation, that depend upon one another.

The embrace of "products" is an expression of a love and respect for images that is the foundation for art therapy's rediscovery of its soul. Moon helps us see the enduring therapeutic function of art—the healing that comes from making objects, perfecting craft, and reflecting upon the images as talismans which change the lives of those who are able to enter into relationships with them. "Faith in the product" assumes that the image has a therapeutic purpose and offers medicine to those capable of opening to its remedies. This shift of authority from therapist to image, threatens the control of the labeling mind which has until recently dominated the modern history of art therapy. Moon reintroduces art therapy to itself and suggests that closer attention to the deep streams of creation that run through our lives will help us realize ways of practicing art therapy that lie beyond our current imaginings.

Many professional art therapists distance themselves from art and strive to become scientists. One-sided identification with science and the repression of the artistic persona produces a malady that Pat Allen calls the "clinification syndrome (1992)." She attributes the malady to a self-defeating inferiority which can be distinguished from the soul-deepening sense of vulnerability and humility that characterize Moon's work. The suppression of art paradoxically makes a shadow of the profession's essence because it threatens the tightly constructed and controlled persona of the therapeutic technician. The primal and unpredictable forces of creation do not fit the guise of the "in control," scientific clinician. This contrast accounts for the hostility that often characterizes the institutional art therapy response to the soulful expressions of therapists who identify with the artist archetype. Unfortunately, this aggression is also addressed to the images and results in the "imagicide" that Moon laments. Images and products are vital parts of the constellation forming the shadow complex of art therapy. If we art therapists do not make, love, and honor our own images, how can we do this for our patients? When will we see that our profession is an ancient and also very new collaboration between art and therapy that presages a transformation of both?

My sense of the shadow aspect of the art therapy is not a matter of "good" and "bad" qualities and it affects everyone involved in the profession. Exploration of the shadow is a mature and deeply affirming gesture not to be confused with the oppositionalism and bickering that characterize efforts to exercise control and power over professional affairs. Moon is not concerned with regulating others or institutionalizing his experience. He simply strives to describe his experience and maintain the freedom to practice according to his personal vision of art and healing. Since Moon works as an artist within a medical environment and collaborates with scientist colleagues, he demonstrates how respect for art does not require opposition to science. However, the power of his medicine comes from his primary identity as an artist who offers something pure and unique to the therapeutic milieu.

The shadow of art therapy can be imagined as the antithesis of the face our profession displays to the world, the qualities that we hide. Bruce Moon articulates how he became caught up in this repression of the artistic persona. As long as the dominant energy of a profession represses a vital part of itself, it is impossible for any of us to avoid collusion until we are ready to openly reveal our discomfort.

Moon says that for over twenty years he denied the ideas that he presents in this book. But the denial is not "his" alone. He carries, lives out, and liberates the collective experience of our profession. The angels and demons of creation are always a step ahead of the reflecting mind. Moon says, "I did not want to hear them, nor did I want to speak them aloud for fear of the repercussions." Just as the individual ego fights against its shadow, the collective ego of a profession guards against whatever it deems unacceptable to its persona. Whoever has the courage to expose and celebrate the repressed shadow can expect an uneven reception. It takes time for these internal inclinations to mature "from inaudible murmurs to clear voices" that Moon offers our profession.

We know from depth psychology that repression of the essential desires of the soul will ultimately generate a primal release of energy. Throughout this book I feel the continuous bursting of the creative essence of art therapy. There seems to be no end to the corrective medicine and Moon models how the transformation of a profession can occur with the precision and discipline that is also associated with the artist's craft. The outburst of passion is paired with aesthetic sensitivity and the containment of media.

This book will inspire serious artists to become involved in art therapy and it will help art therapy students become more demanding consumers who ask, "Where is the art in my training and practice?" The book will also encourage veteran art therapists to renew their vocations by living the process of art therapy which will help us become more effective in reaching others.

Bruce Moon's writing is pervaded by compassion and reverence for the sacred medicine of art. He gives testimony, bears witness, does not try to prove anything, and by so doing makes the book especially convincing and useful. He offers a new paradigm for art therapy practice, a contagious faith based upon personal experience as an artist and therapist. He is not compromised or sidetracked by trying to prove the unprovable. This is a book of inspirations and meditations on the healing function of art in which the shaping of an artistic product is a metaphor for a corresponding crafting of soul. The therapeutic studio is presented as a sanctuary where "confessions, thanksgiving and praises" are expressed through images and where it is all witnessed by the therapist who acts as a caretaker of the environment in which art heals. People are vital contributors to this therapeutic ecology but they step aside to let art do its work.

This homage for the sacred dimension of art therapy reveals yet another of the shadows repressed by the scientist/clinician persona. Moon's affirmation of "faith" is perhaps more provocative than his assertion of art's healing function. He not only challenges secular boundaries of art and science, but mixes the more explosive materials of sacred and profane. Where pre-Freudian society repressed sexuality, the post-Freudian therapeutic world has considered spiritual experience off-limits, thus increasing its shadow power. Bruce Moon, who earned a masters of divinity degree before becoming an art therapist, has never compromised his vision of art as soul's medicine. But I must say that I feel the pulse of the sacred *Imago* in this book like nothing else Bruce Moon has written. By describing the intimate details of how he interacts with his patients, Moon reveals the ministerial function he was destined to serve and affirms his faith in the creative spirit.

The many examples of Bruce Moon's practice at Harding Hospital are straightforward and they show how the making of art will adapt to the person's needs and offer guidance, insight, and revitalization. Art is part of living and Moon repeatedly shows how the creative process cultivates the soulfulness of existence. Love, as Moon suggests, has got everything "to do with it." This book portrays art therapy as an image of the beloved which Moon carries within his soul. The reader who is able to open and become a patient of art's medicine will be transformed as will art therapy itself. This vision of art therapy is an expression of a love for the soul, a love for creation, which is an introduction to art therapy that the profession needs more than ever, a fresh perspective of what we are about which is in keeping with what art has always been. This is what I love about Bruce Moon's work and this book.

SHAUN MCNIFF
Professor,
Lesley College Graduate School
Cambridge, Massachusetts

Reference

Allen, Pat (1992). Artist-in-residence: An alternative to "clinications" for art therapists. *Art Therapy,* 9 (1).

PREFACE

I am never entirely sure where, or when, ideas present themselves to me. They just come, sometimes gently, sometimes fiercely. The ideas in this book have been of the subtle, gentle sort. They have grown, over the past twenty years, from inaudible murmurs to clear voices within. For the longest time I tried not to listen. I denied their existence and their relation to me. I did not want to hear them, nor did I want to speak them aloud for fear of the repercussions they might inspire. Alas, they would not leave me in peace. Gentle as they were, there is a tenacity to them, reminiscent of the dog who will not let go of your pants leg until offered the attention so desperately sought. My cuffs are tattered, but having at last written this book I hope to move about more freely once again.

Over the past twenty years I have worked with mentally ill patients through poetry, drama, music, and sports, but it is in painting and drawing that I feel most at home. I will refer often to the visual arts experiences of my patients, colleagues and students. I embrace and appreciate all of the creative arts and activity treatment modalities, but I am most comfortable in the visual realm.

In some measure this work is a continuation of my first two books, *Existential Art Therapy: The Canvas Mirror,* and *Essentials of Art Therapy Training and Practice.* In *Existential* I laid out a philosophical foundation upon which all my clinical and teaching efforts have been built. This book inevitably bears signs of that earlier work. I was, and am, an existential art therapist. I expect to remain so for quite some time. The focus of *Essentials* was to explore the critical elements of our profession with particular attention paid the role of seasoned practitioners, mentors and educators.

In another sense, however, this book precedes the other two. The content of this effort may be allegorized as the earth beneath the foundation presented in *Existential,* and the atmosphere which surrounds the ideas put forth in *Essentials.* As are so many things in this profession of art therapy, this is paradoxical. This book simultaneously grows from, and nurtures, the prior two. It is an integral notion of mine that most aspects of the art therapy discipline contain and integrate polar ideas, often inspiring conflictual discourse and life affirming struggle. It is fitting then that I write an introduction to the field after the first two texts.

The title of this book, *Introduction to Art Therapy: Faith in the Product,* reflects my desire to explore the prominent dilemmas of our profession. Significant questions of the field will be addressed, but not necessarily answered. I will offer my positions, hopefully in a provocative and evocative manner, but I have no investment in your aligning yourself with my answers. I will feel much more satisfied if you embrace the process of questioning.

The inclusion of *Faith* in the subtitle forecasts my belief that the efficacy of our profession cannot be validated through quantifying methods. Although I am not anti-research, I am likewise not pro-scientification. The heart of my work as an art therapist cannot be measured, nor confined to statistical units. Proof of our professional worth will always be primarily anecdotal in nature from art therapy clinicians, and testimonial from former patients. Neither of these lend themselves to the scientific method. In order to practice art therapy one must have faith in the process, and product.

I have also chosen to accentuate the product aspect of my work as an art therapist by including in the title reference to the artistic end results of our labor. For far too long the products, art objects, that are born in art therapy sessions have been relegated to a subordinate position beneath process. I will make every effort to attend to that injustice in this text.

This book is about the practice of art therapy. It has been impossible, however, to write without reference to education and supervision. These subjects are so tightly interwoven that they have been difficult to disentangle. Perhaps this is as it should be. Yes!

Introduction to Art Therapy: Faith in the Product, begins and ends with discussions of love. These bookends provide the parameters of the work, both in context of this writing, and in the context of clinical art therapy endeavors. Love is the motivator that first called us into the profession. Love sustains us as the work proceeds. I can think of nothing I'd rather have said of me, when I am dead, than that I lived my life in a loving manner.

I hope that this book strikes you as a bit of a jigsaw puzzle. The work that we do is mysterious. It should not be too easily described nor too readily understood. If your reading becomes frustrating, I would ask of you what I ask of my patients, trust me, have faith. I hope the picture will be clear (more or less) when you have finished the book. Until then, struggle with it.

Peace

B. L. M.

ACKNOWLEDGMENTS

I am deeply indebted to many people who have contributed to the writing of this book. Thanks go to Dr. Bob Huestis for his work, *A Psychiatrists View*. Bob's investment in what he terms, "experiential learning," has been a durable source of support and inspiration to me for a dozen years. Special thanks also to John Reece for his chapter, "Dramatic Enactment." John and I have worked together for sixteen years and we've shared a 10′ × 12′ office for the past five. His intelligence is matched only by his creativity and dry wit. Ellie Jones, my retired colleague and editor, has my deepest gratitude for her patience, skill and interest in my work. This book could not have been written without her.

I've been incredibly fortunate these past twenty years to be affiliated with the fine clinical and administrative personnel of Harding Hospital. Most recently, as the entire health care industry has undergone massive change and restructuring, I have felt particularly blessed to receive the constant support of the Hospital community. It has not been an easy time, still I have been given encouragement and freedom to write and work in the manner I see fit.

I must also acknowledge the contributions of Shaun McNiff and Don Jones, H. L. M., A. T. R. At varying stages of my career Don served as my hero, mentor, boss, collaborator, peer and friend. It was Shaun McNiff who first said to me, "Bruce, you should write a book about the work you do." Since that time he has become a good friend and soul brother. Thanks, Don and Shaun.

Finally, I must express gratitude to the thousands of patients I've known, the many students I helped to train, and the colleagues I've argued and celebrated with. They are the ones who taught me most of what I believe to be significant about this profession of ours.

B. M.

Author's Note

The clinical accounts in this book are, in spirit, true. In all instances, however, identities and circumstances have been fictionalized in order to insure the confidentiality of the persons with whom I have worked. The case illustrations are amalgamations of many specific situations. All information regarding patients and clients has been altered and/or fictionalized in an effort to offer realistic accounts of art therapy in progress while at the same time protecting the privacy of individuals.

CONTENTS

INTRODUCTION TO ART THERAPY
Faith in the Product

Chapter I

WHAT'S LOVE GOT TO DO WITH IT?

I ask myself often, "Why do I make art?" I ask my new students the
same question as they enter our graduate clinical training program at
Harding Hospital. "Why do you make art?" So I will ask you, the reader,
"Why do you make art?" Don't answer too quickly. I am not interested in
the answer that comes quickest to mind. There is no more meaningful
question to be asked. For us art therapists this is a matter of bedrock. Our
stability, our place in the therapy world and our authenticity is anchored
to our responses to this question.

Where should I begin? How should I start? Was this book's moment of
conception some time on the morning of St. Patrick's Day, 1967? Have
the ensuing twenty-five years been nothing less than an extended gesta-
tion period? Or did this book really begin to present itself on that April
afternoon in 1991 as I drove through a line of tornadoes on my way to
McComb, Illinois, thinking only that I was going to present a paper at an
art therapy symposium? I had no inkling that my numb death-walk was
about to be exposed. Or it might have begun in that horrible May of '86.
Maybe it was when my mother died last summer? I don't know. I don't
know where to begin.

> *You know I've heard about people like me,*
> *But I never made the connection,*
> *We walk both sides of every street,*
> *And find we've gone the wrong direction.*
>
> *But there's no sense in looking back,*
> *All roads lead to where we stand,*
> *And I believe we'll walk them all,*
> *No matter what we may have planned.*[1]

Don McLean

Morning . . . St. Patrick's Day, 1967. I was a sophomore in High School
in Sidney, Ohio. My life revolved around athletics and rock n' roll. I
liked football and baseball, but lived and died BASKETBALL. On that

3

particular morning I was in gym class. We were being taught the basics of gymnastic apparatus. I was attempting a full flip off the springboard. I didn't rotate completely and landed to the left of the safety mat driving my left heel into the hardwood floor. The pain was instantaneous and blinding. I crushed my heel bone, ruptured the achilles tendon, and that was the end of my participation in organized sports. I never again played on the basketball team. My world view was shattered. How could life revolve around that which was no longer possible? For the next few weeks I was bedridden. For the next ten months I had to use crutches. For the rest of my life I have had to deal with the pain that comes and goes, and the limitations that never alter (Fig. 1).

I entered a deep adolescent malaise. Then came my friend, Cliff Adams, (my first art therapist). Intuitively sensing the struggle that I could not put into words, Cliff began to visit me at home. He was acknowledged the best artist at Sidney High School. I was regarded as a solid guitarist. Cliff offered me a deal. "Bruce," he said, "I'll teach you to draw if you will teach me to play." I was desperate for company and consolation and so our covenant was made. Every day after school Cliff would come to my house and for an hour or so he would instruct me in the proper use of the #2 lead pencil. For the second hour I taught him bar chords and the ten bar blues. In the midst of those dark moments of my young life the arts brought light, comfort and meaning. I survived (Fig. 2).

In the fall of 1990 Ms. Jerilee Cain of Western Illinois University called, asking me to present a paper excerpted from my book, *Existential Art Therapy: The Canvas Mirror,* at a spring symposium that she was coordinating. As I drove I-70 across Ohio and Indiana a line of tornadoes swirled just twenty miles to the south. It was quite a drive.

Over the previous two years I had gradually assumed more and more administrative and supervisory responsibilities at Harding Hospital. My actual time with patients had shrunk to little more than an hour per day. I had no studio art in my schedule at all. In the place of clinical hours were program planning meetings, budget meetings, supervision sessions and a variety of executive committee meetings. The past several years have been exceedingly trying for the health care industry and my non-patient contact days were filled with stress and conflict, both overt and covert. Driving through tornadoes seemed like a perfectly normal thing to do. As I look back on that period of my professional life, I have the sense that I had made myself become numb. I was "just going through the motions."

Figure 1. I've had to deal with the pain.

Figure 2. I survived.

Perhaps because I had no expectations for this symposium... I was just going to present, try to relax and enjoy myself... I was caught off guard as David Whyte, the keynote speaker began his address.

Get up from your bed
go out from your house,
follow the path you know so well,
so well that you see nothing
and hear nothing
unless something can cry loudly to you,
and for you it seems
even then
no cry is louder than yours
and in your own darkness
cries have gone unheard
as long as you can remember...

These are hard paths we tread
but they are green
and we must love their contours
as we love the body branching
with its veins and tunnels of dark earth.

I know that sometimes
your body is hard like a stone
on a path that storms break over
embedded deeply
into that something that you think is you
and you will not move
while the voice all around
tears the air
and fills the sky with jagged light.

But sometimes unawares
those sounds seem to descend into you
and you listen strangely caught
as the terrible voice moving closer
halts
and in the silence now arriving
whispers.

> *Get up, I depend*
> *on you utterly*
> *everything you need*
> *you had*
> *the moment before*
> *you were born.*[2]

David Whyte

It is hard to describe but in the instant that he finished this recitation, something broke loose within me. I felt as if I'd been awakened from a sleep, a long numbing sleep.

On the ten hour drive back to my home I had two recurrent thoughts. I must paint, and I have to get out of the *administrivia* that has ensnared me.

The common thread in these life stories is that they have caused me to think deeply about our profession, about what it is to be an art therapist. They have made me begin to wonder what lies beneath and behind our discipline. Perhaps as a piece of my own *over-forty mid-life struggle* I have questioned my motivation, my push, and the energy that being an art therapist demands. How do we do it? How do we rise from our beds each morning and make our way to work, knowing that our hearts will be shattered as we watch that four-year-old little boy scribble out the pain of his father's belt...knowing that our souls will be battered as we witness the acrylic blood stream down the canvas as that young woman portrays the nightmares that live within her...knowing that our sense of security will be tattered as the seventy-year-old stroke victim offers us images of what waits for us in our future.

What is the source? How do adolescents survive life altering injuries? How do administrators maintain their sanity in the midst of insane health care systems? How do art therapists endure? What is the source?

> *"Everything you need*
> *you had*
> *the moment before*
> *you were born."*[2]

I believe that our source as arts therapists is love.[3] I feel a bit uneasy saying so. Somehow this sounds rather unprofessional, still it is what I believe. I have read numerous art therapy degree program catalogues from the major universities. I have scanned the indexes of many art therapy texts. I have reviewed the art therapists Code Of Ethics. In each instance I have failed to find any direct mention of, or even veiled reference to, love. Still, I affirm that it is this force that motivates us art therapists to do the work that we do. I contend that it is this force which first attracts students into this profession. My belief rests upon this notion, *the doing of art is an act of love.*

I am aware of course that any attempt to explore this idea is an exercise in discussing the immeasurable, illogical and utterly mysterious. No scientific study will validate these thoughts. No legislative body can mandate their truth or falsehood. No form of certification testing can measure the reliability of my assertions. Nevertheless I think that an attempt must be made to grapple with this force for it is surely the foundation upon which all therapeutic structures are built. THE DOING OF ART IS AN ACT OF LOVE.[3]

Throughout the history of the arts countless paintings, poems, dramas, songs and dances have been created solely for the purpose of attempting to describe love. If you listen to popular music on the radio for an hour or so you probably hear, "love," hundreds of times. These modern day expressions range from the romantic to the raunchy, from the divine to the profane. With few exceptions, however, the historic works of art, as well as the current top 40 hits, seem to characterize only facets of love.

The Greek philosophers divided love into three subcategories: agape—divine love; philia—strong attraction; and eros—erotic, sexual love. While this triadic tradition is certainly worthy of deep intellectual respect, it will not suffice for our purposes in this text.

I offer another definition of love. Love is THE WILL TO ATTEND, TO THE SELF AND TO OTHERS. My definition begins with THE WILL TO . . . By inclusion of WILL there is an explicit integration of intent and action. By virtue of my professional history with the range of activity therapy modalities, I am deeply committed to the adage that actions speak louder than words. That love is an *act* of will suggests that it is less an emotion or feeling, and more a manner of being. It is not sufficient to want to be loving, or to feel love. Love must be expressed through actions toward others and oneself. Will also denotes that such actions are done out of free choice. To attend to another is an act of volition. I do not have to love, and I cannot be made to love. I choose to act out of love.

Implied in this definition, THE WILL TO ATTEND TO THE SELF AND TO OTHERS, is a quality of constant dialogue. It is not possible to authentically attend to another if you are not attentive to yourself. In the art therapy studio this principle is manifested through the interactions of patients with their images, arts therapists and their images and the individuals with one another. Being with the images of my patients enhances my capacity to attend to my own creations. Likewise, my familiarity with my work deepens my sensitivity to patient imagery. The same is true, of course, in the realm of human interactions as well. The more comfortable I am with my interior world, complete with its demons and angels, heroic and villainous faces, the more relaxed I will be in the company of my patient's dragons and knights in shining armor. Through this cyclic dialogue a circular artistic process of loving is perpetuated.

Although loving is an act of will, and a choice, the force itself is without goal or purpose. We love for the sake of loving. We attend to another for the sake of attending. We do art for the sake of doing art. Such love brings no increase in personal or professional power or prestige. It brings no material gain. It brings only itself, and that is the most mysterious aspect of love.

The persons who come to the art therapist for help have often been victimized by those who should have been their safest supports. They come bearing their emotional scars, the remnants of physical, sexual or emotional abuse. They have been burned by those who should have loved them. They come hungry for attention, desperate for the soothing balm of love. They long to be understood and held, and yet they are frightened, guarded and defended from the curative effects of being loved.

The creation of art is an act of love. As the artist dips the brush into acrylics and moves pigment to the empty canvas, an image begins its journey from deep within to without. Lines form, shapes emerge, hues enhance and an image is born. This is a process of attending to the soul, so profoundly moving, so full of subtlety, that it resists verbal portrayal. Only the artist herself can experience the full meaning of the unfolding event. My task as an art therapist is to attend, to serve as midwife to the birth. Doing so provides the patient/artist with a restorative, healing milieu. It would be an understatement to define this as anything less than love.

The artist establishes the parameters of her love through the performance of her creative endeavors. She acts out of her love as she creates. The art therapist, through acceptance, praise, or confrontation acts out his love by seriously engaging with, and attending to the art and the artist. The mystery of this creative interaction between artist, image and therapist is that such love is neither earned nor imposed. Creation and attending are acts of grace. They cannot be forced, and they are not deserved. They simply are.

The mystery is felt as the artist steps away from the canvas in order to get a different perspective. It is sensed as others pause in passing to take in the meaning of the creation. The mystery is felt as the artist signs the work, knowing that the signature does more than denote, "I did this." Rather it proclaims, "I am this!"

Being attended to sharpens one's ability to value self and others. Both the lover and the loved see the world with new eyes. As Viktor Frankl said, "Love does not make us blind, it lets us see."[4] All actions and images are enhanced and given meaning through the grace of love. From meaning comes the motivation to create again. From creation comes meaning, comes the motivation, comes the creations and on and on the circle spins.

In, *The Art of Loving,*[5] Erich Fromm suggests that for love to exist there must be five human elements present. They are: discipline, concentration, patience, mastery, and faith. For our purposes in this text I submit that these same conditions must be present in the practice of art therapy. I believe that the relationship between art, art therapy and love is utterly tied to the presence of discipline, focus, patience, skillfulness and faith.

Engaging in any art process requires a degree of discipline. We can never be good, truly good, at anything, if our efforts are undisciplined. This of course implies practice, repetition and struggle. I have often led workshops at universities around the United States. As a part of these intensive experiences I ask participants to work with the same image over several hours. Students and seasoned therapists alike often find this a difficult task. Their lament is that it would be much easier to work on several images rather than to stay with the same one for such an extended period. My response is to gently redirect them to their work, "there is always more that can be done . . . there is always a deeper level to take the image to." I do not take their struggle lightly. I know that it requires discipline to stick with the work, especially when it is not going particularly well, or when it seems as if one has done all that can be done. I know that this is difficult. Still, my insistence that they keep working with the same image sets the stage for all that follows.

Anything that we attempt to do, if we only do it when we are in the mood, or when we feel like it, may be amusing, it may pass the time, but it will never be art. This presents a difficulty in our culture for in large part we have lost our aptitude for self-discipline. Compounding the problem, I believe, is that discipline must pervade the artist's entire existence. It is not enough to apply order to specific tasks, like learning to paint, the discipline must be an ingrained attribute of the whole person. Our culture has become one which deifies relaxation: i.e., time off, time away from the rigors of disciplined routinized work. We have drifted toward a society possessing precious little self-discipline. This deficiency can be seen in a host of sociological phenomena: drug and alcohol abuse, domestic violence, dysfunctional families, the divorce rate, etc. Without self-discipline life is random and chaotic—what Viktor Frankl describes as the, "existential vacuum."[4]

In the arts studio at Harding Hospital where I work, the arts therapists set the tone for disciplined engagement with the arts in many subtle ways. Perhaps easiest to describe here is our approach to the task of painting. Unlike many clinical and educational settings where art therapy is employed, we use no prestretched, pregessoed or factory constructed canvas. From our first encounters with our patients we encourage an authentic and active engagement with materials and processes. Rather than to simply provide the patient with a ready-made canvas upon which to paint, we begin the therapeutic journey by teaching the patient to use the miter saw, cut their own stretchers from 2×2s, and construct the frame. This is followed by training them to measure and cut, stretch and staple their canvas. Applying gesso correctly is the final step in the disciplined process of preparing to paint. I believe that this approach establishes a model of authentic engagement with materials, tools and procedures which inevitably becomes invaluable to patients as they struggle with creative expression. Additionally, this struggle is a metaphor of the intense self-discipline that the patient must apply to the rigors of his or her psychotherapy. If the patient is to find (or make) genuine meaning out of the random chaos of his life, it is critical that he exert control. Without discipline there can be no art. Without discipline there can be no love, and there will be no focus.

It is obvious that focus, or as Fromm described, "concentration,"[5] is an essential element for true engagement in art. Anyone who has ever tried to learn to play the guitar, or taken a ballet lesson, or grappled with watercolors knows that deep concentration is critical. Yet, even more than discipline, focus seems to be an endangered species in our world today. So many things go on all at once. In the span of a twenty minute drive to work I can simultaneously listen to the radio, talk to my wife, eat my Egg McMuffin, and think about the day ahead as well as the basketball game from the night before.

Our culture might best be described as a monstrous, open mouthed, consumer. We have grown used to the visual stimulation first presented to us in the television series, *Miami Vice*, where no picture remained constant on the screen for more than a few seconds. This art form was further refined by the M. T. V. genre music videos. The Presidential campaign advertisements of 1992 used fleeting visual images mixed with sound bytes to create impressions of the candidates. Very little solid information was presented about any one of the three major candidates, George Bush, Ross Perot, and Bill Clinton. Rather, the public was offered glimpses, slogans, and visual sensations.

To be still, without talking, listening, drinking, or doing something is nearly impossible for many people. If there is no focus, there will be no art.

In the therapeutic arts milieu it is the task of the art therapist to monitor the atmosphere of the studio. There are times when interventions are necessary in order to maintain a healthy, disciplined and focused studio. At the same time the milieu must avoid overregimentation for that is the antithesis of spontaneity and creativity.

In my work with severely disturbed adolescent patients one environmental element that requires my continual attention is the playing of music. The radio is, of course, an integral cultural phenomenon for adolescents. At times our having the radio on provides an invaluable connecting point between therapist and patient. As McNiff notes repeatedly in his writings,[6] modern rock and roll music has a primitive and powerful rhythm which stirs our inner creative forces. The music can set the tone for the studio in both positive and negative ways. Sometimes the lyrics, or the musicians' life provide therapist and patient with a common place to initiate dialogue and establish the beginnings of relationship. In other instances the adolescents may turn the stereo volume so high that conversation is made difficult, a resistance to relationship formation. Still other times the music itself is inappropriate for listening to in a psychiatric setting. While I advocate strongly for the freedom of speech in society at large, I have no misgivings about occasionally censoring the music in the therapeutic studio. As an art therapist my first task is to maintain a safe and predictable therapeutic milieu in the studio. The inclusion of music in that environment is at times healthy and appropriate, at other times detrimental. I offer no set rules or cookbook formulas for these issues; rather I suggest that the art therapist be vigilant about all aspects of the arts milieu, continually assessing whether the studio is safe, predictable and comfortable. If it is not, concentration on tasks will be difficult to maintain, for both patient and therapist. If there is no focus, there can be neither love, nor art.

Concentration, of course, demands patience. If you have ever tried to work with clay on the potter's wheel you know very well that nothing is achieved without patience. Learning to throw on the wheel takes time, so much time. It takes time to wedge the clay properly in order to remove all the air bubbles. It takes time to master the process of centering. One must patiently try and try, and try again to insert the thumbs properly in order to open the clay. It takes time to perfect pulling the clay upward. If you attempt to hurry, or take a shortcut through any one of these steps the piece is ruined.

For many people, patience is as difficult as discipline and focus. Our whole way of life fosters and rewards quick results. The computer is a machine revered for its speed. In an instant it can calculate and research data that would have taken hours a few years ago. However, speed is not of the essence when it comes to art and love. In fact, doing these things quickly may be the antithesis of doing them skillfully.

In the clinical setting one of the most challenging tasks that I confront daily in my work with severely disturbed adolescents is that of helping the patient learn to slow down. The arts provide a wonderful action metaphor for this aspect of the patients treatment. There are simply some aspects of artistic processes that cannot be hurried. For example, the raw canvas must be gessoed. The gesso must be allowed at least a few hours to dry thoroughly before the next phase of the painting process can proceed. My patients often express frustration with this aspect of their treatment in the creative arts studio. I try never to miss these opportunities to comment on the nature of the arts, therapy, and life itself. I will respond to my anxious patient, "Well, you're going to have to let the gesso dry for the rest of this session. Why don't you use the time to think about what you are going to paint, or you might want to make some initial sketches to plan your painting."

Patient: "But I want to paint today."

Bruce: "I understand, but some things just take time, you can't hurry this or you'll make a mess of things."

Patient: "Can't I start as soon as the gesso is mostly dry?"

Bruce: "No, you really have to wait until it's completely dry. That way the canvas will be entirely sealed and will hold the colors better."

Patient: "But I really thought I'd get to start painting today. I don't want to think about it any more and I don't like to sketch. I want to paint.

Bruce: "You know the Rolling Stones said it best, *you can't always get what you want.*[7] Sometimes it's important to take your time, be patient."

Patient: "I don't like being patient. I want what I want when I want it."

Bruce: "In art it just doesn't work that way. You have to cooperate with the materials and procedures. That's sort of like life you know."

Patient: "This is boring."

Bruce: "Do you know where boredom comes from?"

Patient: "What are you talking about?"

Bruce: "You said you were bored. I believe boredom comes from an absence of quality relationships. If you have good relationships in your life it doesn't matter where you are, or what you are doing, you are never bored. On the other hand if you don't have quality relationships, you could be at Disney World and be bored. Do you see what I mean?"

Patient: "What's that got to do with art?"

Bruce: "Well, good relationships take a long time to grow. You have to be patient with them, they can't be hurried. That's the same with doing art, you can't make the gesso dry faster than it will. You have to be patient."

Perhaps the most controversial of these essentials for arts therapists relates to the notion of skill, or mastery. Fromm asserts that the artist must be ultimately concerned with mastery of the task.[4] If the art . . . if the therapy . . . if the loving is not of ultimate concern, the novice can never really learn it. One may be a dabbler or hobbyist, but never the master. I regard it as crucial that my students, and patients learn to shade, drybrush, layer and wash. By doing so they experience themselves as capable of stopping, rethinking and struggling with the process. This is a particularly difficult element to grapple with for art therapists. Why?

Much of the literature of our profession has argued that the PROCESS is of the utmost importance in the therapeutic use of the arts. The

PRODUCT has received relatively little press. Through such teachings the role of mastery has been downplayed in service to expression. I am no longer convinced that this is wise. It may be an example of our collective fears regarding our artistic proficiency. Perhaps we suffer some unconscious product phobia. Or it may be the result of our living in a culture that does not particularly value the arts, process or product. Regardless of why we have so shyly dealt with the element of mastery, I believe that it must be reclaimed as an essential characteristic of our profession.

This assertion often stimulates heated discussion as I teach and lead workshops at universities throughout the United States. The complaint most loudly voiced by students is that they do not regard themselves as *ARTISTS.* I am never entirely sure how to respond to these student reactions. At one level I don't understand why someone would enter training for the profession if they did not feel some measure of competence as an artist. I would never regard myself as an accountant, for I loathe numbers and mathematical procedures. But, implicit in my selection of art therapy as my profession is my underlying love for the arts processes and products. Secondarily, I wonder if the students complaints regarding my assertions that we must be artists, that we must exhibit some forms of mastery of media, are born of a misguided sense of what it takes to be an artist. My response to them is always the same, "There is no magic that determines that one person is an artist and another is not. The only genuine route to mastery is practice."

My son Jesse loves basketball. He has worked very hard to become good at the game. He shoots extremely well and is adequate at most other aspects of the game. This is no accident. He has practiced and practiced. Still, when he went out for the basketball team as a seventh grader he did not make the final cut. I was out of town the night that he was cut and when I called home to get the news he cried on the phone. I ached for him. By the time I got home two days later he was back outside at our hoop practicing again, working toward next years try outs. Jesse understands the essential nature of artistry—mastery and PRACTICE.

Unfortunately all too many people in our time have lost touch with the ability to struggle. Many art therapists I have met lament that they cannot paint. I mourn the fact that they do not struggle or practice. Rather, they give in to the frustration of "failed" efforts and avoid the pain of future deficiency by ceasing the activity. Nothing that is valuable comes conveniently or easily. As art therapists we must reclaim our identity as artists who are ultimately concerned with both process and product.

Each of these four elements: discipline, concentration, patience and mastery, depend utterly upon the necessary requisite of *FAITH*. The practices of art, art therapy, and love demand faith. By this I mean that we must have faith in the goodness of life, the arts, of others, and of ourselves. Fromm said, " . . . only the person who has faith in himself is able to be faithful to others."⁵ I would emphasize that only the art therapist who has faith in her, or his, own images is able to have faith in those of others, i.e., clients. I would add that if we have no faith in the power of images we have no reason to be in this profession. This is why I am so disturbed when I hear a colleague bemoan the fact that they never do art for their own sake anymore. They complain that there is just too little time, that they are too busy . . . too tired . . . too . . . too.

At every stage of my life, at least since St. Patricks Day, 1967, my art has comforted me when I was in pain and afflicted me when I was too comfortable. #2 lead pencil drawings helped me survive the life shattering injury to my left foot. The words of a poet awakened me from a numb administrative death walk. Now, rather than one hour of patient contact per day, I log more than twenty hours per week, most of it in the arts studio. A painting forecast my mothers death in 1991 (Chapter XXIII, *ESSENTIALS OF ART THERAPY TRAINING AND PRACTICE*).⁸ It prepared and strengthened me and accompanied me as I became no one's son.

Every little boy must have someone to look up to. A man, by his very being, shows the boy what it is to be a man. In the best of situations this initiation is done between fathers and sons. My father died when I was just eighteen months old. In his place, in my eyes, stepped my sister's husband, Marvin. As I grew up Marvin was always special to me. He was big and strong and not afraid of anything. He played football, built houses, helped me build soap box cars. Marvin took me fishing, and taught me to hunt. One memorable afternoon in 1962 he explained how men and women make love (Fig. 3).

In the time that I was growing up Marvin built two houses for his family. I have vivid memories. The first one was constructed when I was four or five years old, but I remember carrying pieces of wood, sweeping up, doing whatever I could to please him. I recall how badly his words stung as he nicknamed me "Lightning," because I wasn't moving as quickly as he wanted me to.

Figure 3. He was big and strong and not afraid.

By the time he was building the second house I was a teenager. He gave me my first real paying summer job, helping him build. What a summer that was. I drank my first beer one hot July afternoon. The other men on the job told their off-color jokes as if I was just one of the guys, not a kid anymore. Marvin was always larger than life.

In 1987 Cathy and I built our house together. I nearly burst with pride when Marvin showed up on the first day of construction and praised the work I'd done on the main support beam. It was perfect! I have a photograph of him and me placing the last log at the peak of the roof. He was there, he was always there.

About a year or so ago Marvin was diagnosed as having leukemia. A variety of medications have been tried but he continues to weaken. Blood transfusions help but the intervals between them continue to shrink. He is fading, withering before my eyes. I know that he will die soon. Perhaps not this year, maybe not next, but soon . . . soon. We will build no more houses together.

What can be done? How can I bear this life as it is? I must paint, and I must love.

Why do I make art?

Why do you make art?

I have no choice. What's love got to do with it? Everything . . . everything. Have faith! (Fig. 4, 5).

Figure 4. Building the house.

Figure 5. Building the shed.

Chapter II

THERAPIST OR ARTIST?

In 1975, at my first American Art Therapy Association national conference, one of the first presentations that I attended dealt with the question, "Am I an artist, or a therapist?" It has been so long ago now that I don't recall who the presenter was, but I do remember that my internal response, though kept to myself, was that this was an odd question. Throughout the intervening years this same question has often been the source of spirited debate whenever two or more art therapists gather to exchange ideas. I believe that at one time or another I have heard each of the "PIONEERS" of our profession express their views for or against one particular stance or the other. My mentor, Don Jones, A.T.R., H.L.M., consistently held the position that he was first and foremost an artist. Don's authenticity in this has been validated since his retirement in 1988. He now spends much of his time painting and sculpting, doing what he has always said was most important for him to do. Many of his contemporaries held fast to the opposite view, i.e., they saw themselves as therapists first who have a special affinity for using the creative arts in a manner beneficial to their therapy work with clients.

In 1975 I kept my reactions to the question to myself for I was, after all, a neophyte. Still, my answer has never changed. When I am asked by students or colleagues today whether I consider myself an artist or therapist, my response is always, YES. When the questioner shakes her head and asks again, assuming that I must have misunderstood her question, I answer again, YES. If pressed to explain myself I begin by stating that I believe the question to be inappropriate. How can we be anything other than both? Is it not doing violence to each word of our professional title to separate them as if to dissect? We must be reminded that only dead things are are dissected. Is asking the question an assault upon the life breath of the discipline itself? To be sure, taking apart the words of our title, breaking them into their separate parts, is a typical western, lineal thinking thing to do. This is flawed thinking that is needlessly divisive.

The question lives on however. At a recent A. A. T. A. national conference much attention and debate was leveled at the variety of roles arts therapists play. Among these faces of the field are artist, educator, clinician, healer, administrator, shaman, archetypal psychologist, researcher, and supervisor. In the stimulating and provocative discussion that followed one panel presentation, a member of the audience asked the panel to comment on her assertion that although she considers herself to be a competent art therapist, she does not consider herself to be an artist, nor does she desire to be one. The panel members responded in a sensitive and appropriate manner given the circumstances. I had a very different reaction to this woman's position. Had I been able to talk with her after the presentation I would have liked to ask her why she entered the profession. It is imperative that art therapists be artists. It is vital also that we be knowledgeable therapists. These roles must not be separated, one from the other. Although semantically unusual it would be helpful to our professional identity if we could describe ourselves as ARTTHERAPISTS.

The roots of this long standing divisiveness are traceable to the inherent arrogance of many persons who describe themselves as artists, and the pomposity of many who bear the title of therapist. Perhaps it is human nature but both of these camps have an ample quantity of vocational conceit. I have had the good fortune to function in the separate realms of each. For nearly thirteen years I taught at a professional arts school. In that setting I was often confronted with the vainglory of both faculty and students In that culture there is a caste system that places the fine arts practitioners at the top, advertising personnel at the bottom, with illustrators and fashion designers spaced in between. The fine arts people believe that they are the only true artists in the school, while the advertising people smirk to themselves that the "fine artsies," will have a rude awakening when they go out into the real world and try to make a living being creative and clever. The hostility among these various factions is usually covert, yet never far from the surface.

The tragedy of this caste system is that the sub-groups miss many opportunities to learn from one another. Occasions that could enrich their learning are often avoided out of fear of contamination.

In my role at the college I often sensed much mistrust from my arts colleagues. In a faculty meeting one of my peers told me that he thought that the other faculty members were frightened of art therapy because it ascribes meanings to art works that go beyond media and technique. I have no way of ascertaining the validity of my peer's statement, yet I suspect there is at least a grain of truth in what he said. In *Existential Art Therapy: The Canvas Mirror,* I suggested that, "Artists have always known that a major source of their creativity is their own inner emotional turmoil."[3] If I am correct, it is understandable that the art community would be reticent to fraternize with art therapists; their fear is that we might intrusively analyze or interpret their works as stemming from inner disquiet.

I have more extensive experience dealing with the psychological treatment community. In this sphere there is also a caste system, though it generally tends to be clothed in civility. Within this system psychiatry sits atop the pyramid of power and prestige (perhaps with psychoanalysts hovering just above the pinnacle.) The psychiatrists are closely followed by psychologists, who are followed by social workers. Depending upon the specific institution there is then a layering of nurses, adjunctive therapists and other technical specialties, with aids and attendants at the base of the pyramid. Generally speaking, members of each stratum are rewarded commensurate with their station in the system. I have always found it fascinating that this system works in such a way as to *discourage contact with the patient.* By this I mean that those persons at the very bottom of the pyramid, the attendants, spend the most actual time with the patient yet are paid the least. Conversely, the psychiatrist often spends less than one half hour per day with his patient, yet is paid the most for his efforts. This would seem to be a systems flaw, or corruption of Freud's intent foreseen in his comment, "Everybody thinks that I stand by the scientific character of my work and that my principle scope lies in curing mental illness. This is a terrible error that has prevailed for years and that I have been unable to set right. . . . in all countries into which psychoanalysis has penetrated it has been better understood and applied by writers and artists than by doctors."[9]

Perhaps at some deep unconscious level there is an awareness on the part of the medical community that artists were the prototype analysts. This would explain why, in many settings, members of the psychiatric profession regard art therapists with a measure of discomfiture. It is the art therapist's comfort in dealing with the deeply disturbing imagery of the patient that inspires a veiled disciplinary rivalry which is publicly unacceptable, which psychiatrists do not like to admit to themselves.

The arrogance of the psychotherapeutic community is expressed in many ways. Foremost among them is the expressed belief that they know how to do therapy more skillfully, more effectively, or more efficiently than anyone else. This happens within different segments of an institution, as well as between competing centers of care. For instance, I consulted with the activity therapy department in a psychiatric hospital for a period of six months. In that facility the adolescent division of the hospital was convinced that the adult division didn't know how to treat inpatients correctly. The adult division felt that members of the adolescent division were overly controlling and heavy handed in their approach to treatment. This rivalry seriously effected the members of the activity therapy department. They felt that they had to choose up sides, idealizing one approach while devaluing the other.

At the same time, members of both divisions vociferously argued that their institution's standard of care was far superior to that of a competing hospital across town.

So it is that the art therapy community has inherited a tradition of hubris from both of our ancestral professional roots: art, and psychotherapy. This tradition is maintained as students come into the field from one direction or the other.

I suggest that we must appeal to the higher natures of our lineage. Artists have always had a unique creative capacity to integrate polarities in their work. "The creative act is the transforming agent of powerful conflictual forces within the artist."[3] Through creative, transformative actions we may be able to forge a collective identity inclusive of all the disparate faces of our work.

Therapy, in its root form, means *to be attentive to.* Surely this implies the ability to attend respectfully to our differences in service to our commonalties. Art therapy is significantly more than the actions of sensitive humanitarian artists. Likewise it is immeasurably more meaningful than the techniques of verbal psychotherapists who dabble with crayons and markers in their clinical work. It is the marvelous covenantal relationship of art and therapy that fuels the powerful work we do. Each aspect embellishes and enhances the other. The absence of either diminishes both.

When I am asked, are you an artist or a therapist? My response is always the same, YES! I hope that this will be your answer as well.

"As an art therapist, am I primarily an artist or therapist?" At the 1992 A. A. T. A. Conference in Las Vegas other nuances of identity confusion were added. Scholars of the field discussed the adjoining roles of educator, clinician, and healer. Still I believe that the fundamental question that shapes the professional personality of art therapists is the preexistent, *am I an artist first, or a therapist?*

This is a critical and essential question for it addresses the soul of the discipline. It approaches the matter of where we art therapists came from and, I believe, our answer to it defines who we are, both as individuals and as a professional community.

It is difficult to pinpoint just where, when, and by whom art therapy was first utilized. Some would argue that our roots go back as far as the ancient cave paintings of Lascaux, France. Others point to early writings by Freud that mention the imagery of his patients. Certainly Carl Jung was a significant thinker and practitioner of psychotherapy who had the highest regard for the role of the arts, both in his own life and in his work with patients. Still others credit Hans Prinzhorn with bringing attention to the art of the insane, thus stirring interest in the formal use of the arts as a therapeutic agent. In this country there are "pioneers" of the profession who seem to have spontaneously arrived in the occupation in the middle of the 1900s. Irrespective of where, when or who, there seems to be a consistent high regard for images and art processes and products.

It is from such regard for image, process and product that I posit the belief that art therapists must regard themselves as artists, first and foremost. It is a fascinating conundrum to me that art itself, materials, process, product and history receives so little attention in art therapy academe.

To be sure, the trek of the art therapy graduate student is a complex one. It travels many paths simultaneously. One path is filled with books, articles and lectures. Another is littered with powerful emotional experiences unlike anything the student has undergone before. There is yet another path—an inward one defined by the images that emerge within the student as they brave the educational journey.

It is difficult to understand why so little attention has been given to the art aspects of our collective persona. I often hear colleagues complain that they have no time to paint or draw anymore. I counter these lamentations with the notion that one always has time for what is really important. I seldom have too little time to hug my daughter or play basketball with my son or kiss my wife. Likewise I make time to engage in art making.

This is more than just a matter of semantic interest. It is a matter of professional survival. At the time of this writing, 1993, it is a difficult period for all clinical disciplines in the mental health fields, I have known many social workers, activity therapists and art therapists who have either lost their jobs, or left them of their own volition, due to the extremely unfavorable financial climate surrounding health care in America. I have heard art therapist friends say that they wonder sometimes if they made the right decision, when they chose the field of art therapy as their life's work.

I can in good conscience say that I have never had such misgivings about my vocational decision. Yet I am not immune to the insecurities regarding employment future that plague everyone in uncertain financial times. I particularly worry about the prospects for my students. Still, this does not alter my resolve to be an art therapist, for I feel secure at my foundation, THE ART. I know that to do art is good, I have faith in the product and the process. My anchor, in the turbulent world of the psychiatric hospital, is my own art. The images which come to me as a result of my contact with the art of my patients deepens and enriches my life. The only times when I have felt the numbness of being "burned out" have been those times when I, for whatever reason, have strayed too far (too long) away from my studio. I believe that in an existential sense I could live without being an art therapist, but I do not think I could survive without doing art.

When my students ask me for guidance regarding their prospects for employment security in the future I respond to their questions in the most authentic manner I can. "If you stay active as an artist, you will survive in this profession. If you give up the doing for your own sake, you may, in all likelihood, depart from the field if things become too difficult.

My position on this fundamental question is clear. One must first be an artist, in order to become an art therapist. Art is the anchor, the soul, the tap root of the profession. "ARTIST: one who professes and practices an imaginative art." (Websters New Collegiate Dictionary.)[13] This does not imply that one must exhibit his or her work, or enter competitive situations. Rather it leads to a definition of the art therapist as one who practices an imaginative art and attends to others through the process and the products of artistic work.

Chapter III

WHAT IS METAVERBAL THERAPY?

For most of the history of the art therapy profession writers and theoreticians have been comfortable with defining the discipline as a non-verbal treatment modality. I, however, am not satisfied with this description of our work. I am apprehensive that this portrays the work negatively. Doing so can be interpreted as a defect in our corporate identity. It is imperative that arts therapists define themselves positively, i.e., what we are, rather than what we are not.

The definition of art therapy as a meta-verbal treatment modality is much more suitable for our purposes here. *Meta*, is a prefix meaning, *beyond*. Through this description, art therapy is a treatment modality which is *beyond words*.

I am certain that the essence of our work as art therapists is found in the interaction between patient-artist, media, procedure and therapist. Whatever we say about this interaction in no manner changes the nature of the process. The heart of the profession is experienced in moments that defy verbal description. Our words serve only to verify (for the therapist) the messages of the interaction. They do nothing to change the meaning itself. In a fundamental and revolutionary sense, I believe that the most important work we art therapists do is done without speaking at all. Every time I find myself talking too much in an art therapy session I worry that I have lost my center, both as an artist and as an art therapist.

I have practiced art therapy for twenty years in an institutional setting, and for five years in a small private practice. In all that time, having treated thousands of patients and clients, I recall no occasion when the referring therapist, or the patient, sought my services because of my reputation as a verbal therapist. On the contrary, patients have been assigned to me, or have sought me out because of the need for a meta-verbal treatment approach. The extraordinary gift that art therapy has to offer our clients is that the arts provide a psychotherapy milieu that is not dependent upon words. Relationships are forged by doing, and art is what we do. The world of therapists is heavily populated by disciplines for whom words are the primary, if not the only communicative device. Psychiatry, social work, psychology and psychiatric nursing all depend upon verbal exchange with the client. The arts therapies represent a therapy of imagination, refreshingly distinct from our verbally oriented colleagues.

It is in this spirit that I challenge all art therapists to be skeptical about their longing to talk meaningfully with the patient. I do not mean to imply that I am silent in the creative arts therapy studio. I am likely to talk with my patients about the weather, or the basketball game the other night, or who their favorite musician is. I may in passing discuss the art show that I attended over the weekend. I may struggle out loud with my own artistic work in progress, and I often share my reactions to my patients' art. Still I do not see these interchanges as anything more than they are, pleasantries. The real work . . . the soul work, has happened before any sounds in the shapes of words pass my lips.

The arts provide glimpses of the inner lives of my patients and of myself. Every paint streak, each chalk line, every slab of color, harmonious and dissonant, declares to the artist themselves, to the beholders of their work and to all humankind that *I am, I am here and I have something to express.*

As for the audience, conceivably the most it can do is to catch a fleeting glimpse of the multi-layered communication of the creator. From such glances come the first stammering attempts at dialogue between beholder and artist. As we art therapists look at the works of our patient/artists we must wrestle to uncover and focus the feelings, thoughts, physical effort, and the soul of the piece. We must always engage an art work as if it were a sacred icon, the symbol of a holy story. As mysterious as this may sound, every time a patient pulls color across the canvas a proclamation is offered to the world, *I am here, and I have something to show you.* Too often in my patient's lives the responses they have received from such declarations have been indifferent or malevolent. It is a dangerous thing, TO BE. It is beyond words (Fig. 6).

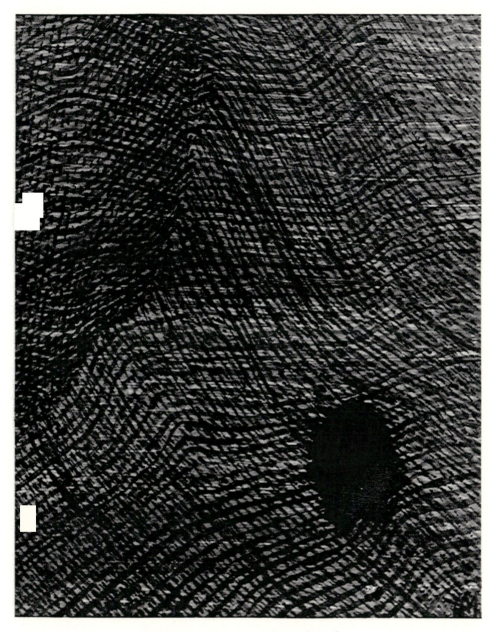

Figure 6. The image is beyond words.

Chapter IV

WHAT IS THE NATURE OF THE WORK?

I'd been on vacation for three weeks. It was my first day back at the hospital and as I walked into the creative arts studio I was aware of Jenny's hostile glare. Out of the corner of my eye I saw her squirt a long stream of white glue onto a piece of masonite. She randomly placed mosaic tiles on the board, paying no attention to color or design.

I approached her, "Hello, my name is Bruce. I've been on vacation for awhile, who are you?"

She turned toward me, one fist clenched. "What do you care?" This inspired a round of snickers from her peers.

One of the other adolescent patients said, "This is Jenny, she came in last week."

"Thanks," I said. "Now Jenny, what are you working on here?"

She shoved the masonite my direction without speaking.

"What is this about?" I asked.

Jenny turned to her friend, "What is he talking about," she smirked.

"I'm talking about what the theme of your work is. We want artists to work on important things in this studio. You know, things like feelings, or events, that have been significant in your life.

"You want me to draw a PIG?" She snarled.

I learned later that she had been sent to the hospital from the juvenile court system. She had several serious criminal charges, pending psychiatric evaluation.

"No," I said, "But I...."

Jenny glared at me. "I don't give a shit what you want."

"Jenny, you're going to have to not talk that way in the studio. We need this to be a safe and comfortable place for everybody. Swearing makes it hard on everyone."

"Are you fuckin' for real?"

"Jenny, I'm really serious about this. Now can we talk about your art work?"

She grimaced. "It's nothing, I'm just doing it."

"Well," I said, "we'll have to start something that has meaning for you. I'll stop back in a few minutes." I turned and went back to my own painting.

As I started to work at my canvas I overheard Jenny sneer to her friend, "I can't do a damn thing with him bitching at me."

"That's it, Jenny. I'm calling the unit to send you back. We really can't have talk like that out here. We'll try again tomorrow."

The next day went much like the first session had. She was again sent back to the unit for being negative, devaluing and hostile toward me. As she was leaving the building I told her, "Tomorrow let's build a canvas together and get going on a painting."

To my surprise Jenny entered the studio the following day and announced that she was ready to work. I began by showing her how to use the miter saw to cut 2 X 2s for her frame. She whined that the wood was too hard, and the saw too dull. My response was, "Jenny, struggle with it."

After the frame was built I taught her how to stretch canvas. She asked, "Could you leave me alone? I can do this."

"All right," I said, "but let me know when you get to the corners, they're tricky."

When she called me back to the room where she'd been working I saw a too loose, too wrinkled canvas.

"Jenny this isn't tight enough. Let's take it off and start over."

"What?" She groaned. "It's Tom's fault. He came in here talking to me and . . ."

"Jenny, there is no substitute for paying attention to your work and taking your time."

"Why isn't this good enough?"

I began pulling out her staples. "Because you are worth more than this. C'mon, give me a hand."

"I can't do this," she exclaimed.

"I have faith in you." I replied.

"I can't do this," she protested.

"Trust me," I said.

I watched, during the weeks that Jenny was in the hospital, as she learned to cut, hammer, stretch, gesso and paint over, criticize, re-work and finally sign her canvas. The image is of a desert plain leading to a desolate mountain range against an empty magenta sky. It is an intense, lonely image, a poignant metaphoric portrait of Jenny.

What is the nature of the work that we art therapists do? It is painful, emotionally bruising and blistering, stretching and demanding. No one seeks therapy because of feeling too good. Therapy is sought most often as a last resort, when all other avenues for alleviation of discomfort have been tried. Therefore the work is not often reflective of happiness, fulfillment, or peace of mind. More times than not the guideposts of therapeutic work are rage, loss, hurt, abandonment, anxiety, guilt and emptiness. The roads these guideposts delineate are hard to travel. The seeker has been forced upon them through life's circumstances. The patient is wary, guarded, hesitant to trust, and quick to lash out. It is on these paths of anguish that the first steps of the therapeutic journey are taken. The therapist must not be put off by the resistances of the patient. This is how the patient begins to tell his story. It is not pleasant, nor easy, nor comfortable work. There have been many Jennys in my professional life; kids who are filled with loathing for adults and for themselves. Rageful, lonely and damaged souls forced to emotionally fend for themselves in a world all too willing to abuse their vulnerability.

In the treatment of severely disturbed adolescents like Jenny the first and foremost task is to set clear, consistent boundaries in order to establish a safe and predictable milieu. It was natural for Jenny to resist and distrust me. All of her life experience with adult authorities led her to believe that I would in some way be harmful to her. It was important, therefore that I respond in a neutral affective manner, establishing the boundaries of our relationship and setting clear limits on her self defeating behaviors. Although it was not a pleasant task to confront Jenny's resistive behaviors, it was a necessary one.

It is the nature of psychotherapy to contain a phase of resistance. Art therapy is not immune to this factor in its initial sessions. No one, child, adolescent, adult or geriatric, seeks therapy when feeling good. The act of entering therapy is an acknowledgment that life is painful. Even when the client has volunteered and is anxious to begin the therapeutic journey, still it is human nature to resist involvement with pain. Despite all the good intentions of the art therapist, the patient cannot help but identify him with the pain of life. It is the nature of the work to deal with the resistance of the patient.

The working through phase of therapy is marked by a significant decrease in overt and covert resistance maneuvers. Like the first phase, the working through stage is often not put into words. Most often it is observed in the behaviors of the patient. This is a time of intense work as the patient begins to exchange negative self-concepts (introjects) for the more positive views of self that coming from encounters with the therapist. As patients experience the art therapist's positive regard, his genuine interest and his ability to understand and honor the patients' pain, they begin to rework their internal sense of self. As the art therapist encounters the battered and bruised inner world of the patient and responds in a way that is different than others in the past have done, the patient's self-regard is altered. The essence of the curative process is the patient's awareness of being understood. Inherent in this understanding is the belief on the part of the patient that, despite the ugliness, the monsters, and the horrible feelings that she harbors within, the art therapist still accepts and cares for her, just as she is. The art therapist's unique ability to understand comes from the capacity to be with, and attend to, the images of the patient.

Jerry was a wild kid, a terror, everyone said so. He was eleven when I first met him. I'd read his hospital chart and I knew about his past. He'd been abandoned by his mother, left in the bathroom of a bar when he was a year and a half old. He'd been shuffled around the foster care system, spending time in eleven different homes before he was adopted. Though his adoptive parents had all of the best intentions toward Jerry, his monstrous behavior had so frightened and alienated them that they were considering giving custody of Jerry back to the county childrens service. Adopted at the age of five and a half, he'd made their lives miserable for the last eighteen months, prior to hospitalization. He'd been aggressive at school, eventuating in his being suspended several times. He'd set fire to the curtains in his house, causing thousands of dollars of damage. He ran away, he sometimes wouldn't talk for days at a time, and at other times he would not be quiet. Jerry was a wild kid . . . a terror.

He'd been in the hospital for about three weeks when I received a request from his physician, asking if I would evaluate him to see whether or not he might benefit from individual art therapy. I met with him for a forty-five minute initial interview and was immediately fascinated by his images and his rage. In the evaluation session I offered him a range of artistic materials and told him that he could make whatever kind of a picture he wanted to make. He gave me a sidelong glance, as if to ask if I was serious. I assured him that he could use whatever materials I had in the room and that he could draw or paint whatever he wanted.

He quickly gathered all of the tempera paints and arranged them on the table before him. He asked, "Can I paint on that black paper?" He pointed toward a roll of black construction paper leaning in the corner. Again I assured him that he could use whatever materials he wanted.

Jackson Pollack and the Peanuts cartoon character, Pig Pen, would both have been proud of Jerry's efforts that morning. When he finished, the studio was a disaster. Paint was everywhere. He titled his work, *The Blob Man.* He said, "This is what I see when I close my eyes at night."

The image that Jerry created was chaotic, confusing and overwhelming to look at. Upon the black background he had swirled rivers of red, purple, brown and blue. Over these he had poured streams of yellow and orange. Finally, as a crowning touch, he carefully dripped countless beads of white and gray. As I went about the chores of cleaning brushes and paint cups I sighed, "It must be hard to sleep with all that going on."

"Yeah," he said. "Sometimes I hardly sleep at all in the night. But don't tell my mom, she'd be mad if she knew." Then he spit onto his painting. "So can I leave now?"

I turned toward him, "Yes Jerry, you can go if that's what you want to do, but I wouldn't mind it if you wanted to help me clean up." To my surprise he picked up a wet sponge and began to work on the paint splatters he'd made on the work table.

Nothing more was said during that session, but by the time we'd gotten the studio back into proper condition I felt relatively sure that I could work with Jerry, and that he could (and would) use the art therapy process.

In the months that followed there were many tests of my patience and determination. Everything from Jerry's past had taught him to be suspicious of adults. He had no desire to be hurt again and so he exhibited a host of resistance behaviors.

The psychiatric team that was responsible for planning and monitoring Jerry's hospital and out-patient treatment developed an understanding of his difficulties as stemming from early deprivation, both physical and emotional, and the trauma of abandonment. Our working hypothesis was that his emotional development had been stalled somewhere around the level of a two-year-old. This phase of development is characterized by the child's emerging sense of independence, need to separate from the primary nurturer, (mother) but frequently return to her for emotional support and security. It was the sense of the treatment team that Jerry had never been able to move past this early stage since he'd had such instability in his relationships with caregivers. We theorized that this developmental arrest accounted for his aggressive behaviors directed most often at parental figures, and situations symbolizing movement away from the primary care giver, i.e., school.

From this understanding we formulated a treatment plan designed to provide Jerry with multiple reparative experiences intended to help him work through his early trauma and to stimulate developmental progress. We had no illusions that this would be an easy or quick cure. Jerry's difficulties were serious and his resultant coping behaviors were a nearly life-long pattern. Compounding the problems in this case was the fact that Jerry was only eleven years old. To expect him to be able to work in individual therapy based primarily on verbal exchanges was unrealistic. A regimen of action-oriented psychotherapies was ordered for him.

Jerry was in the hospital for eight or nine weeks. This provided him with a safe, predictable and emotionally neutral containing environment. All therapeutic disciplines; recreation therapy, music therapy, play therapy and educational tutoring, reported a gradual decrease in Jerry's resistances as the weeks passed. As he became increasingly cooperative and trusting of the staff his defensive distancing maneuvers faded. He was discharged from the hospital with a plan for on-going art therapy and play therapy weekly sessions. He had begun the working through phase of his therapy.

Jerry was sitting at a table in our large creative arts studio working on an acrylic painting. The scene he was trying to depict was of a dark room. He wanted there to be two doors on one of the rooms walls, each standing open revealing long hallways. He had just completed painting a silhouette of a human figure huddled on the floor in the corner of the room. He slammed his brush on the table and exclaimed, "This looks like crap, Bruce."

I turned from my easel, lay down my palette and went to his side. "Hmmm. I see what you mean, Jerry. I think it is the person. You only used black. Everything else in the picture has colors. I think the black looks out of place."

"I don't mean just that. This whole thing looks like . . . "

I interrupted, "It would probably work better if you tried to make the pants the color of old blue jeans. Maybe you could have the shirt be the color of your *Laker's* shirt." I picked up his painting and placed it on the easel I'd been using. I stepped away a few feet, then called him to my side. "Yes, I think that will work Jerry. You've really got an interesting piece going here. The hallways give it an eerie and lonely feeling." I returned the painting to his place at the table. "Let me know if you need any help with the purple for the shirt. I think I'd start with the indigo and add just a touch of white."

"But I can't do this." He lamented.

I went back to my painting, smiled at him and said "I have faith in you Jerry. I'll help you when you need it."

Without further comment Jerry went to the paint cabinet and gathered his colors. Later in the session he asked for help mixing the maize that he wanted for the trim on the *LAKER'S* shirt. It was my sense that he did not need my assistance at all, but I had provided a way for him to get the emotional support that he needed.

Variations on this vignette were experienced over and over and over again. These interactions were the essence of the curative process for him. It was crucial that I offered him opportunities to work independently . . . to metaphorically toddle off and explore the world. It was likewise critical that I be there for him when he returned to my side for emotional support.

In order to understand the significance of this interaction, imagine the toddler who leaves the room where mother is working. He goes to the playroom, occupies himself for several minutes, then realizes that he is alone. He makes his way back to mother in order to insure that his world is secure. The mother stops what she is doing, bends down, smiles and coos, gives the child a hug, and he is off to explore the world again.

During the working through phase of therapy, Jerry, metaverbally, experienced these toddling situations repeatedly. Each successful venture served to form the foundation of his capacity to resolve the developmental fixation. As he became more resilient and self-assured his aggressive behavioral reactions to his adoptive parents and school authorities diminished.

It is important that the reader understand that therapy at this level is not, cannot, always be put into meaningful verbal constructs. Jerry had to learn by doing. That is the nature of the work.

It is obvious that this second phase of the therapy process is the most gratifying for the art therapist. It is in the working through that changes in patient behavior and self image are seen. It is here that the individual is able to view his life as a story he has a major part in writing. He takes responsibility for his difficulties and successes equally. All of these aspects make the working-through phase of treatment appealing to the therapist. Yet, it must be stressed that such work is not possible without the earlier struggling with resistances. Likewise the accomplishments of the working through phase are left incomplete and hollow without a poignant period of termination.

It is essential that art therapists understand that termination is a process, not an event. The termination phase of therapy is a critical one, for it is during this period that the patient is able to demonstrate the solidity of changes made. This is a period of increased anxiety. It is often experienced initially as an abandonment. If the therapy has proceeded ideally the patient has come to trust the art therapist, feel cared for and safe. It is easy to understand how the approaching end of the relationship is interpreted as a cancellation of a covenant.

The early stages of the termination phase are often marked by temporary regressions as the patient struggles to cope with the anxiety and loss related to saying good-bye to the art therapist. This anxiety is exacerbated if the therapy has taken place in a hospital or residential treatment facility, for not only is the patient leaving the art therapist, he is also saying farewell to doctors, nurses, activity therapists, social workers, and peers. Ambivalent feelings are prevalent. On the one hand the patient can't wait to get out of the hospital, back to his normal life. On the other hand he has formed significant relationships, had experiences he will never have again, and hopefully feel better about himself than he has in some time.

In the two decades that I have been involved in therapeutic work I have observed thousands of patients terminate. This process can be characterized by four dominant patterns or metaphoric themes.

1) *I will get mad at you, you will be angry with me and I will feel no pain when I leave you.*

The meta message underlying this style of termination is that the patient believes it will be too painful to say good-bye, to really let the therapist know how he feels about her. This is fairly typical of adolescent patients for whom acknowledgment of their feelings, especially warm/dependent ones, is often difficult in relation to adults.

It is critical, when dealing with patients in the termination phase of treatment who manifest this style of coping, that the therapist not allow herself to be cast aside by the patient's anger. Rather, it is imperative that she respond in a way which honors the anger, as well as the pervasive fear of loss which engenders it.

2) *I will withdraw from you early, so that when I leave I will not miss you.*

The meta-message here is a belief on the part of the patient that if he is out of sight he will be out of mind. His withdrawal is often misunderstood as being a rejection of the therapy experience in toto. In this instance it is important that the therapist not become overly solicitous, rather she must remain accepting and responsive to the patient's imagery and behavior, yet affectively neutral.

3) *Wasn't this wonderful, I'm so glad I met you, you've really changed my life.* Patients coping with their anxiety in this way are falsely glorifying their treatment experience as a way of defending themselves from the reality of how difficult life post-treatment will be. There is often a magical wish that now that they have sought therapy, their lives will be forever smooth sailing. This is of course, never the case. By assuring treators that they have done a wonderful job in helping, they keep the focus off of the difficulties that lay ahead.

4) *I will use this time to honor the work that we have done together.* Those who are able to use this form of the termination process take the opportunity to summarize the work that has been done in the context of the therapy relationship. This approach to the process of saying goodbye is marked by realistic recounting of the meanings created between patient and therapist. There is no effort, on the part of the patient, to either glorify or devalue the importance of the relationship. This authentic engagement in the ending process is generally viewed as a positive prognostic indicator.

There are several notable sign posts which mark the productive therapeutic journey. The art therapist must be vigilantly looking for these as the pilgrimage unfolds. In order for therapy to be successful the patient must navigate through the resistance phase. The skilled art therapist knows that this is being done when the patient is able to take ownership of his difficulties without undue blaming of others for his misfortunes. One of my art therapy students described this in the following way; "It's like the patient had been watching his life on video tape, suddenly he realized that it was more like a play, and that he was the playwright."

The working through phase is discernible as the patient becomes interested, not only in self-disclosure and introspection, but in meaningful behavioral change as well.

Finally therapy, like all things, must come to an end. The fruits of the work are harvested as the patient is able to define the significant qualities of his relationships, including feelings, perceptions and meanings. It must be stressed here again that this may, or may not, be a process that is put into words. In the hospital setting, more times than not, such things go unspoken. They are however, acted out symbolically through drawings, paintings and sculptures. This is the nature of the work.

The Story of Jan

When I first met Jan she had the striking good looks and poise of a young professional model. I wrote about her hospital art therapy in my first book (pp. 64–66). "Jan had been raised in a well-to-do family. She said that everything she wanted had always been hers for the asking. To the outside observer she had everything that should have made her happy. Her family loved her, all her material needs were supplied, she had an exciting life . . . and yet Jan had tried to kill herself. That brought her to the hospital and into the art therapy studio. . . . A few weeks into her hospitalization, Jan began to paint. After several aborted attempts at portraits, still lifes and landscapes, Jan was dejected and frustrated. She asked to have her daily schedule changed so that she could be entered into ceramics and withdrawn from creative arts. Jan and I agreed that she would leave the studio after she had completed one painting. She was irritated by this delay and asked, sarcastically, 'What do I have to paint, Boss?' Without responding to her subtle hostility, I suggested she work on the theme of *good-bye*. I told her she could use any style she wanted, but it was important that she finish it."

"What emerged as she worked was strikingly different from her other clumsy attempts at mimicking someone else's style or reproducing a photograph in acrylic paint. She began by painting the entire canvas a dark red. She covered the bottom half with black and, leaving a sliver of intense red, she painted the top portion a deep indigo. The effect was powerful. The red pulsated behind the darker colors, evoking the image of a wound. Here at last was a work, not sugar-coated or blemish free—a raw, painful expression of the inner self. . . . On the day she signed the work, I asked her if she wanted to talk about it. She said no, she just wanted to stretch another canvas and get to work on her next painting. I went in search of the staple gun."[9]

I'd had no contact with Jan for two years or so since she'd left the hospital until her psychiatrist called one afternoon to inquire if I would see Jan in my private practice. I had fond memories of our work together and I agreed to meet with her early the next week to explore the possibility of renewing our treatment relationship. Jan's doctor informed me that she had been married and divorced since last I'd seen her. The marriage had been an impulsive one, and unhappy from the beginning.

He said, "They made a beautiful couple, they just didn't like each other very much." He also informed me that Jan had initiated his contacting me, and that he was feeling frustrated with her because she was so often flippant and superficial about her life. It was their hope that she might be able to engage more seriously in her therapy through involving, once again, in the art processes.

Jan came to my office the following Tuesday. After getting reaquainted we began an artistic pilgrimage which lasted for nearly two years. During that time Jan worked on painting after painting, each new one delving deeper than the last. It was as if the art process formed a metaphoric onion for her. Each new creative act peeled away another level, revealing ever more precious aspects of her complex self. Images of beauty and beastliness gave way to raging inner fires. These were quenched by deep sorrowful pools which in turn evaporated beneath a harsh inward sun that baked a barren desert. Layer after layer, image upon image the prismatic person that she was beneath her flawless shell emerged.

As her inward pilgrimage unfolded I had to do very little. Jan did all the hard work.

The author, James Hillman, writes, "A Particular image is a necessary angel waiting for a response."[10] Jan was greeted by many angels in the years that she came to me for art therapy, and respond to them she did.

She'd been attending sessions regularly for about twenty-one months when she brought a painting of a chalice sitting on a bench in front of an old small town train depot. She had restricted her palette to gentle umbers and warm, subtle yellows and oranges. The image had a dusty forlorn quality.

As she worked on this painting she mused that it reminded her of the small town in western Ohio where her grandparents lived. She recalled taking a train ride to Lima, Ohio with her grandpa. She said that she'd always wanted to stand on the wooden walk in front of the depot and greet some long awaited visitor as they arrived on the train.

"Jan," I said, "I wonder what it would be like to get on the train and head off into the sunset?"

"You mean be the one that was leaving the people at the station?" She asked.

"Yes," I replied. "What would that be like?"

She grimaced. "I don't know. I never leave anyone. They always leave me."

Jan was fairly quiet for the rest of that session. She asked for technical help on one small section of the piece, but I believe she did not really need my assistance. In the silences I was aware that something had passed between us during the interaction around the train station, but I was unclear just what it was.

I took my notes from the session to my next meeting with my supervisor. I described the eerie silences, reconstructed our conversation as best I could and tried to portray verbally the painting Jan was working on.

When I'd finished telling the story he asked me how I felt. I told him that I had a warm, yet lonely feeling. "She must be telling you that she's almost ready to terminate therapy," he said. As soon as his interpretation had been made I knew that it was correct. I asked if I should raise the subject with her at our next session. He suggested that I maintain the neutral stance that I had adopted during the course of her therapy. "She'll put it into words, or pictures when she is ready to."

When she returned to my office the following week she brought only her sketch book. I inquired as to the whereabouts of the painting and she remarked in an offhand manner, "I forgot it."

The painting continued to be, "forgotten," for the next two sessions. It reappeared on a bright afternoon in late October. Jan had added highlights to the chalice and roughly sketched the figure of a man standing on the boardwalk beside the tracks. Although the drawing was quite hesitant and lightly done, it appeared as if the man was waving toward the vanishing point between the two rails on the distant horizon. "Ah, I see you've been working." I said.

"Yes. I had this sitting in my dining room for the longest time. I hadn't touched it. Then, the other night I got the urge to add the man there," she pointed.

"He's waving?"

"Yes, he's been left behind," she sighed.

The rest of the hour long session was spent in casual discussion of painting techniques, an art show that had recently opened at the Columbus Museum of Art, and how things were going for Jan at work. At the close of the session, as I was filling out an appointment reminder card for her Jan said, "Could we not meet again until two weeks from now?"

"That would be fine. Are you busy next week?"

"No," she said. "I just thought I'd like to try coming a little less often for awhile."

Two weeks later Jan called my secretary and cancelled our session. She scheduled an appointment for the following week.

When she arrived for the session the painting was in much the same condition it had been in three weeks prior.

"I've felt stuck," she lamented. "I can't seem to get his arm right." She pointed toward the upraised waving arm of the man. "Could you stand up for a minute and pose like that while I sketch it again?"

I turned toward her. "I've wondered if maybe that figure wasn't supposed to be me." Jan offered no reply. She focused her attention on the canvas before her.

"Ok," she said, "I'm done drawing, you can sit down."

"You missed last week."

"I know, something came up." Nothing more was said for several minutes. When I approached the easel where she was working I could not help but notice that the figure in the painting seemed to have clothing similar to mine.

Jan put her brushes in the water container and sat down. "Yes Bruce. I think the guy in the painting is you. I think he's waving good bye to me."

I shifted my gaze to the painting. "I wonder how he feels, waving good bye?"

(This style of dialoguing with the image was quite familiar to Jan, so she easily slipped into the imaginal discourse.)

"Oh I think he's sad and happy both."

"How is that possible," I asked.

She paused. "He's sad because he won't get to see the woman on the train very often anymore. She's moving away. And he's happy for her too, because she is happy."

"I see. Where is she going?"

"She's moving out west, to Colorado."

I quoted Paul Simon, "Everybody loves the sound of a train in the distance, everybody thinks it's true."[11]

Jan shifted her weight on her stool. "I think it's about time, Bruce. I think I'm ready to move on" (Fig. 7).

"Everything ends, Jan. Your painting is a beautiful symbol of endings. Maybe we should talk about your stopping therapy?"

"I think I'll just paint."

Over the next few weeks the painting continued to grow. Details were added. She painted an easel behind the window in the depot, a symbol of our time together. A faded circus poster was added to the weathered wall

Figure 7. I think I'm ready to move on.

of the station, recalling a particularly difficult period of Jan's therapy in which she felt herself to be false—a painted clown. For the most part Jan and I spoke of artistic techniques, shadows and light, washes and highlights. Still, the painting became a symbolic object, an icon of sorts, representing our relationship. Images of pain, sadness, anger, loneliness joy, and finally hope emerged. It was, in dramatic fashion an imaginal map of our journey together. Several times Jan wondered out loud what I would do if she, "just disappeared." At each of these moments I reminded Jan that in my view saying goodbye was a process not an event.

Our process ended as Jan signed the painting. It is, for me, both a haunting and warmly nostalgic piece. As she spoke of it during our last session together she recalled moments of poignancy and silliness that had passed between us.

I have wondered, from time to time, how Jan is doing in her new life in the West. I hope that all goes well for her, she deserves good things in her life. Now and again I feel as if I am a professional goodbye sayer. It is almost frightening to me to think of how many significant relationships I have established over the past two decades only to bid them farewell. It is the nature of the work. The whole point of establishing the therapy relationship is to make it no longer necessary.

My friend, Jim Lantz, once said to me that, "the whole of life is captured metaphorically in the first few seconds after birth. The baby is cast out from the warmth and symbiosis with the mother during the birth process. Within seconds the child is placed back upon the mother's belly. This is, in an emotional sense, the story of the rest of our lives, negotiating our separateness and connection to others."

Yes!

Chapter V

DRAMATIC ENACTMENT

John Reece is an Adjunctive Therapy Supervisor at Harding Hospital and a faculty member of the Clinical Internship in Art Therapy. In his clinical work with adult and adolescent patients he has used music, poetry, horticulture, recreation and drama as therapeutic modalities.

Prologue

My role is that of the interviewer, hers is that of the newly-admitted psychiatric hospital patient. The setting is a meeting room of a short-term adult unit.

I introduce myself and tell her that the purpose of the interview is to gain information from her that will enable me to recommend a program of therapeutic activities. She nods her understanding, and so I ask her about the difficulties that led to her hospitalization.

Helena is a large, florid woman in black, tight-fitting clothes. Her makeup is overstated and she is wearing conspicuous jewelry. At my question, she looks startled, then gazes out the window of the meeting room for long seconds. "I just couldn't take it any more," she states in a small voice, and tears spill down her cheeks.

She begins a monologue that lasts more than forty minutes. It includes three unfaithful, alcoholic husbands, four ungrateful children, her sainted mother, backstabbing co-workers, one loyal and many untrustworthy friends, and a granddaughter who is perfect and the only reason Helena is alive right now. At different points in the interview, she clasps my hands and stares searchingly into my eyes, pounds a fist on her knee, weeps openly, laughs ironically, and asks questions that she then answers.

As an interviewer, I am to remain neutral and observant; as a caregiver in mental health, I am to be receptive and empathic. Despite these imperatives that define my role, thirty minutes into Helena's monologue, I find myself distant from her. I appreciate her well-rehearsed performance.

49

I note the details of her costume. I easily liken her story to the plot of a sad, overblown soap opera, a real weeper. I am completely out of character.

At this moment, Helena looks deeply into my eyes and clasps my hands.

"Yesterday, my sister told me my life is just like a soap opera. Isn't that the most heartless thing you ever heard?" Helena begins to weep again.

Introduction

Dramatic enactment is the most commonplace art form. Each person engages in it and most of us practice it daily. It is an art form freely interwoven with social interaction on every level and in every possible circumstance. Because of this, it is often invisible as a form of art and substitutes for real life. It is the ultimate *trompe l'oeil*.

Dramatic enactment is a preplanned, even scripted interaction; the fulfillment of a role; the identification of the comic and tragic in real life. All aspects of the theater can be and are woven into everyday life's fabric. Each of us plays roles, directs others and is directed, writes and recites dialogue. Each of us rehearses and each of us spends time to find our motivations and to get into character. We all hit our marks and say our lines. We all seek and love applause.

I am enacting dramatically when I:

- Ask Bruce how I should approach our boss for a raise;
- Cheer on Becky when she tells the story of a recent triumph;
- Put on a suit and tie to look more professional;
- Discipline Cherie, an adolescent patient with a history of abuse, in a fair and non-abusive way;
- Internally applaud Helena's superb dramatic skills in retelling her tale of woe;
- Stop applauding Helena because it is not professional to do so;
- Make a wisecrack in a dull meeting;
- Plan what wisecrack to make and look for an opening;
- Decide that the meeting needs a wisecrack and that I am the person to deliver it;
- Act interested in the meeting when actually bored stupid;
- Or, in bed at the end of a day, review the day's events and the way I behaved, evaluating my performance, and previewing the events of the day to come, make plans for tomorrow's behavior.

In the examples above, I function as actor, director, audience member, playwright and stage crew. Without much effort, I can see my whole life as a series of entrances and exits, rehearsal and performance, script and improvisation. If I were to choose to see my life this way, it would become practical fact. I have known people whom I assume have made such a choice.

It is possible to engage in dramatic activity and be unaware of it. The forms of drama are compelling and the means of enactment often subtle. Human society has a long historical relationship to theater and all of its aspects are archetypal in the collective unconscious. People naturally think of events in terms of stories, people as characters, conversation as dialogue and listeners as audience. This thinking is so natural that it becomes automatic, so automatic that it becomes unnoticed.

Thus, a person who has chosen to see life as drama may do so without awareness of that decision. To abide by a decision that you are unaware of having made is to severely restrict your ability to change that decision. This has crucial therapeutic implications, as we shall explore later.

Not all action is dramatic enactment. This is true in the sense that not all sound is music or all movement dance. There must be intention to engage in the art form. A person who behaves in a spontaneous (unrehearsed) way is not engaging in dramatic enactment. It is possible to imagine a person living out a life in such a way, not preparing or reviewing, not attending to the audience, not overtly directing—or preparing, attending or directing in a way that can be called dramatic. One might think of a Zen master, a shaman, a *brujo,* a prophet, The Man with No Name. Such persons have a distinct air of unreality about them. That is because drama and reality have been so long related and mixed that to subtract drama is to subtract part of reality, too. People expect (without being aware of the expectation) other people to perceive and behave in dramatic terms.

Dramatic enactment, as an everyday, semi-invisible art form, serves a vital purpose to humanity. It provides a structure for understanding. Truth (reality) is stranger than fiction because it is less comprehensible. Humans need to interpret raw reality to make sense of it. Art forms of all kinds have this critical mission. Patterns and structures from the arts codify and simplify the stream of data called life. An artistic view is a "take" or perspective that suggests a meaning.

In the end, the purpose of art forms is to enable the expression of human values. Moralistic stories and propagandistic art make values explicit, but there is an enactment of values in every artistic gesture. This is at the core of the omnipresence of art, including dramatic enactment. Each dramatic decision, gesture, response, review, rehearsal, direction—is guided by, and in the service of, the values of the one who enacts them.

Art, Artifice, Artificial

One of the reasons dramatic enactment in everyday life is an underground event is that it is suspect. Rehearsing and directing have much in common with plotting and manipulating. While it is certain that a person will enact their own set of human values, it is not assumable that they will act in accordance with another person's values or societal values. A scam always involves stage business. A swindler always portrays a character. Criminals rehearse. Cheaters act innocent. As Jiminy Cricket laments, "What use has an actor for a conscience, anyway?"

For this reason, a person often hides his or her dramatic actions and insists that such actions are those of a spontaneous, guileless person. Adults are almost universally embarrassed when asked to perform dramatic skits and part of this embarrassment is pure sham. It is itself an act to suggest that I am so natural and spontaneous that dramatic enactment is totally foreign to me. The actual part of this embarrassment is that I will be revealed as a skilled actor although I maintain theatric innocence.

To reveal my practiced dramatic self is to expose my artificiality. Though all humans traffic in posturing, dissembling, role-playing and enactment, it is a considerable risk to admit one's false, constructed self. Part of the fear in this risk is linked to either/or thinking in the form of: if I am false in any aspect, then I am a false person. While this fear is irrational, it contains a core of truth.

An artificial, constructed reality can never stand substitute for actual experience. To the extent I substitute my own dramatic constructions for reality, I separate myself from reality. It is possible to overdo dramatic enactment and thereby live in an uncomfortable, false and separate world. The sincere part of Helena's pain is the pain of separation. Real intimacy cannot tolerate the playing of constructed roles. A person who is unable to suspend roleplaying is unable to experience intimacy. Dramatic enactment is an art form that people are essentially required to participate in. Nevertheless, an authentic human experience, one that includes intimacy, requires that a person be able to disengage from the process.

Most people work hard to hone their dramatic skills. While this work is usually cast in a different light—as assertiveness, conversational skill, etiquette, being a "people person"—it is in fact a refinement of an art form.

A person has an estimation of his or her own relative artistic skill level in the dramatic arts. A shy or regressed person has an accurate view of his or her lack of dramatic skill and therefore shies away from social interaction the way a poor pianist avoids playing in public. Helena has considerable dramatic skill but overreaches her talent—an overestimation that probably prompted her sister's remark as much as her circumstances.

Dramatic enactment in everyday life is not commonly seen as the art form it is. It is commonly ignored or seen as something else. Yet it exists and furthers the goal of any human art: to make life more understandable and to express values. Pervasive and important as it is, it remains an artistic commentary on life and thus does not, and cannot, encompass the whole of human experience.

Dramatic Enactment in Therapy

Many human problems can be viewed as bad theater—failure of the dramatic enactment process. As Berne (1972)[12] insightfully illustrated, people in therapy have been given bad scripts. His views reveal the machinelike determinism in tragic life. His therapy, called "Script Analysis," was devoted to the recovery of one's script from the unconscious and to rewriting the script in less restrictive terms.

The assumption of a tragic, destructive script can be seen as the worst possible outcome of a dream-for-life substitution. Script Analysis began its work by correcting the central error. It calls bad drama just that. It enables the patient to make decisions from a position outside the script—a director and not the helpless actor.

Much of my work with patients aims at their awareness of choices they didn't know they had. In my mind, I always frame such awareness as the dramatic metaphor of empowered director replacing encumbered actor. The actor, strutting and fretting poor hours on the stage is unaware that his or her life is a story subject to rewrites; that an improvisational change of action can accomplish a story change. This, in the realm of drama, is akin to what Bruce describes elsewhere in this text as the artistic process of shifting from the role of the victim to the position of the hero through creative work.

As stated earlier, a person can make a choice to substitute dramatic forms for actual experience, and then be unaware of having made the choice. This is the tough nut of tragic script. If the dramatic forms chosen are destructive ones, the person actually lives a painful life based on a central mistaken assumption. Hasn't every treater wished to shake a patient awake, to intrude from the wings of the stage? Therapists all have a visceral experience of a patient's tragic determinism—a repeated march toward destruction. My hatred of this determinism is its utter needlessness. It only continues because the patient believes that he or she is only an actor compelled to play out a script.

Therapists frequently gain a view into real-life melodrama, with sweeping, multigenerational scripts and large casts. A hospital admission is seen as just this week's episode; when discharged, the client/ character will return to the story in progress to play out the predetermined role. The process of therapy, which therapists regard as crucial, even sacred, is relegated to some minor onstage business. Therapy is doomed years before it started, because the patient in your office or studio is living out a victim's role in a saga that needs a victim for dramatic balance.

In view of such powerful forces, what is a therapist to do? It is typical for the treater to teach the victim some non-victim actions, to have the victim rehearse some non-victim lines. Also typically, the victim dutifully studies these new behaviors in the therapy context, then swiftly abandons them back home. Sometimes a therapist arranges for the victim to leave the drama, move out of a home and start a reconfigured life in a new, unwritten script. And just as predictably, that patient will find a way back into the old role and script, or will uncannily recreate the story with new actors playing old roles. (In fact, I have often seen such patients auditioning other patients and staff at the hospital for these roles.)

The patient, though in pain, returns to the pain-causing patterns because the patterns are enmeshed in the only reality the patient knows. To abandon the only show playing in your town faces you with the terror of the unthinkable. The dramatic form of your tragic script was long ago substituted for your actual experience of events. Because the purpose of the dramatic enactment is the expression of values, the patient's playing of his or her role, however tragic, is what gives meaning to life. My colleague, Darlene Norman, and I have long discussed the "nugget of truth" that lies at the core of every patient's pathology. To me, it is that patient's belief in the meaningfulness of the role he or she is seeking to perfect. The patient's truth is a sensible truth only in the context of that drama. The patient clings to pathology because it contains truth.

Therapeutic empathy means that you, the art therapist, understand the drama that is being enacted in your patient's life and see his or her role in it. You then use your own dramatic skills to project yourself into that role. You understand the motivations for the actions your patient performs and the lines he or she speaks. Your patient's "nugget of truth" becomes your own.

Empathy is usually spoken of as an important element in gaining the patient's trust and acceptance, engendering hope. These things are all true. And the trust is rewarded, and hope justified, when the therapist takes the next step in empathy. The therapist remains in the patient's character and *then* examines options and choices for changing the drama. Therapeutic options obtained this way have such greater power because they represent the choices the patient might conceivably make.

It isn't possible to overstate either the difficulty or importance of the process just described. The primary human challenge for the therapist is to allow myself to assume a value system that is not just different from mine, but perhaps in conflict with it. Because my value and belief system underpins my own sense of reality, I may feel threatened to my core to suspend myself from it, even for a short time. Unresolved identity issues in the therapist are inevitably played out in the therapeutic relationship because of the demand that the therapist suspend his or her own character to assume the client's own. The therapist's relative failure is proportional to the inability or unwillingness to perform this empathic character switch.

When the therapist is unable to establish empathy, the result is two individuals viewing and using each other as objects. The patient feels like a thing that things are being done to. The therapist is in a state of pure frustration, unable to see the slightest progress. Because of empathic failure, the therapist tends to blame the client for the therapeutic failure — and this blaming widens the empathic gap.

A patient who desperately needs to connect with a therapist under these conditions may accept the role seemingly offered by the therapist: the antagonist, a relationship-destroyer. Too often, the patient is too well prepared for this role and enacts it with a vengeance. This scene may be played out over many years and many different therapy situations. The client's assumed role, reinforced by long practice, solidifies. This patient who now comes into a new therapy situation (and this will happen because the core problem has never been addressed) has the primary task of doing violence to the new therapist's efforts to help. My term for this hardened role is "treater beater."

Another common sequel to empathic failure is apathy and separation. The eventual outcome is that the patient drifts away from therapy unhelped while the therapist is vaguely relieved that the frustrating patient is gone. The unfortunate result of this circumstance is that the client's sense of hopelessness is reinforced as well as any other character elements that represent relational failure. The therapist, too feels and must accommodate a disheartening self-view—perhaps as an inept treater or an inadequate human being.

It is the bleakness of the outcome of empathic failure in therapy that demands that the art therapist take the risk of empathy. But what is to be done about the legitimate fear of identity loss? Art therapists, being human, have unresolved issues in the core of their identities. A therapist is likely to have a complete or partial lack of awareness of these deep issues. That means that a particular issue will sneak up on the therapist and present itself in full flower, as terror, at the delicate moment of attempted empathic connection with the patient. What to do?

Engage in the art form. Act. An experienced actor knows, from repeated experience, that he or she can assume the most threatening, demanding role and survive it with original identity intact. It is the sense of artistic mastery that can carry the art therapist through the empathic terror. The empathic connection established by the therapist based on the mastery of dramatic (and artistic) techniques is not "just an act." It is a sincere *artistic* gesture. Art joins humans together on the most fundamental, unspoken level, the level of the archetype and the collective unconscious. My work as a therapist is my art. The particular variety of art is dramatic enactment.

Clinical Vignettes

I have chosen to attend to the subtle art of dramatic enactment in my interactional day. I believe that my conscious decision has enriched my awareness of human experience be enabling my empathy. My engagement in the drama (the art) is not that of the passive audience member, but more like that of a responsive and responsible member of an improvisational theater troups.

It is the nature of my job, as an adjunctive therapist, to wear many hats and to perform various roles. It is perhaps worth noting that in the differing situations I will describe, I always carry my awareness of the dramatic aspects with me. I am always "on," as a conscious choice.

In the following brief scenes, I will sketch out action and dialogue from therapeutic episodes. Then, in a discussion, I will show some of the ways the art of dramatic enactment describes and affects that scene.

Vignette 1. Russ

Russ, a middle-aged farmer, approaches me at the beginning of a horticulture therapy session and asks "Well, what's on the agenda for today?"

I have just finished giving task assignments to two other patients. "That depends," I tell him. "What do you want to do?"

There is a pause. "Whatever needs to be done," he eventually replies. "You're the boss."

"I'm not, either", I argue, "I'm your employee. You're paying me." Russ stares at me wordlessly, with a fixed smile. Within five minutes he has begun to follow the student intern, silently helping her with tasks.

Discussion

Russ was admitted following an unsuccessful, serious suicide attempt by poisoning. The role Russ seems to have assumed in life is that of a hardworking, opinionless man whose family sees him as simple and rather negligible. The tragedy in Russ's character is that he is passionate and strong beneath his passive drudge mask. Repeatedly and historically thwarted in his attempts to assert himself by his powerful, controlling mother, Russ finally only wishes to assert his fundamental human dignity and exit the stage on his own terms. But even that attempt was a pathetic failure, Russ having been accidentally discovered by his brother with the poison container to his lips.

Russ has been given a crappy role in a melodrama. His script seemed to demand that he trudge passively and compliantly through psychiatric treatment, making no waves, then upon discharge return to his unchanged tragic home life to seethe within and concoct a more efficient suicide plan.

In the scene described above, Russ attempts to assign me a role familiar to him—a boss, someone who directs him without caring, who sets agenda without input. My response confounds him. The rejection of a role in improvisational drama is serious business. You don't do it without a reason because it exerts pressure upon your fellow actors. I chose to exert this pressure on Russ because I saw absolutely no purpose in enacting the role he was auditioning me for. Unfortunately for me, Russ's story had no other characters in it. There was Russ and there were uncaring, controlling abusers. Russ felt the discomfort of the pressure I applied surely enough and he responded to it as a new form of abuse. Apparently, in Russ's view, a psychiatric hospital is where they abuse you with brain games. In responding as I did to Russ, I had elevated my role from simple tyrant to psychological torturer.

And there I remained, stuck in a bad role in this wretch's drama. Russ's melodrama was so blatant and confining that every attempt I made to develop or redefine my character was cast as further incomprehensible abuse.

I was not satisfied with the resolution to this drama. At the end of our scenes together, Russ shook my hand blandly, said goodbye tonelessly and gave me a tight smile that said: Finally rid of you, you son of a bitch.

Vignette 2. Emily

"I'm HERE, I'm HERE!" Emily strode into the woodworking studio. The adult patients stopped their work to look at her; her teenage peers went on sanding and painting without a glance. "Where the HELL is my project! Oh, HERE it is! Who the HELL put it HERE! Come here, my little baby!" Emily kissed the wooden car.

After a few minutes, when she was sanding loudly but not talking, I said, "You know, Emily . . . " then trailed off. I studied a paper pattern on the table.

"What?!" she demanded.

I paused, then spoke in private tones. "I was just thinking about a drama therapy group I used to do here. If it were going on today, I'd sure want you in it."

"WHY?" Her lip was curled in a sneer. Her eyes blazed challenge.

"Because I believe you have a lot of natural talent."

"What the hell do you mean by that?"

"I'm not sure. It's just a feeling I have." I looked at her mildly for a few more seconds then moved on to another conversation. The rest of the woodworking session was quieter.

Discussion

Emily was always bigger than life. It is often difficult to ascertain the stability of a role played by an adolescent, because it is in the nature of adolescence to try on many roles, playing each different one to the hilt. But Emily showed an adult-like consistency of character over the weeks that I knew her. She was almost universally melodramatic at the top of her lungs.

From a theatrical point of view, bigness is an attribute; Emily was born to play the larger houses. The fact that she hadn't yet found an appropriate venue was a function of her youthful inexperience. That she chose to magnify her childishness and dependency with her talent was a function of her psychiatric problems.

In the episode above, I rather blatantly addressed her inexperience as a dramatic enactor and ignored other issues. Her relative quietude following the exchange was a pleasant side benefit.

Vignette 4. Annemarie

It was a group designed to help patients improve their communication skills by the practice and application of a few easily-understood techniques. Annemarie entered the room downcast and the pleasant pregroup chatter died. She sat down slowly and deliberately, meeting no one's eyes. The uncomfortable silence was broken by a question spoken in a small voice. "Are you okay, Annemarie?"

Annemarie did not answer nor did she look up. The silence pounded our ears. I began to prepare a few standardized introductory remarks relating to the purpose of the group when Annemarie spoke.

"I guess y'all should know I'm havin a bad day." There was a long pause. "They told me I should come to group and maybe deal with it. This is the anniversary of my father's death. He was the one who abused me and I can't get over that. He's dead." Annemarie looked up and met each group member's eyes in turn. "How'm I supposed to deal with that in here?"

There was another long silence. Abruptly Annemarie stood up and strode to the room's exit. "I knew this was a farce," she said, and exited stage left.

Discussion

Annemarie's acting skill was extraordinary and she matched it with impeccable timing and staging. Her forte was underplaying, the essaying of a role from beneath. Her performance was an iceberg, the spoken words the only tangible part to suggest the great moving weight in invisible depths. The accomplished underplayer establishes an unseen emotional conduit to the audience member, so that you squirm in your seat, feeling the feelings she is studiously not displaying on stage.

In clinical talk, this is "projective identification," a process that boggles the logical mind unless understood as a theatrical process. It suggests that the patient can engender her feelings in you while they remain unexperienced by her. This sounds like voodoo, not psychiatric science. But I've never heard a treater experienced in personality disorders dispute the existence of the phenomenon.

The underplayer knows what the expected symbols are and then merely suggests them. It is akin to a great artist's minimal pencil sketch that suggests the coast of France with three squiggles. Annemarie had built her role brick by brick in the days preceding the scene above. She was famous at the hospital. Almost everyone knew who she was and what her issues were. And a significant number of people, treaters and patients alike, felt responsible for her emotional comfort and well-being. Annemarie was the hapless victim that controlled everything. When Annemarie ain't happy, ain't nobody happy.

In the scene above, she wreaked her vengeance on an unjust, cold world by destroying a therapy group session. Following her exit, the remainder of the group was spent, worrying about Annemarie and comforting the weeping group member who asked her if she was okay. As it turned out, Annemarie was fine. The anniversary was ten years old. Annemarie was a treater beater on the pro circuit. She beat up whole groups.

Epilogue

Annemarie and I had a few individual discussions following this episode, in which I asked her to consider the group as not directly helpful to her. Instead, I suggested, she might use the group as an opportunity to reach out and help others by giving them feedback on their communication.

What I was proposing was that she assume a different role in the group. Believing that she loved controlling her roles, I was pleasantly surprised that she agreed to do this. I was not at all surprised that she had a wealth of knowledge about communication upon which to base her feedback. She was obviously a master communicator.

As artist-therapists it is your task to pay close attention to the drama your patients engage you in. You must be willing to regard all aspects of your work as art-form-in-process. You must attempt to understand the role the patient has cast you in, and you must improvise as you strive to help the patient understand that they can write a new script. It is not only the painting, the sculpture, the poem or the dance that is the art form in the therapeutic context. Every word you utter, every move you make and each facial expression you display are pieces of character in the dramatic enactment of art therapy.

Chapter VI

TRUTHS AND FICTIONS

METAPHOR...

fr. L. metaphora, Gk. fr. metapherein to transfer, meta + pherein to bear. 1. a figure of speech in which a word or phrase literally denoting one kind of object or idea is used in place of another to suggest a likeness or analogy between them (as in the ship plows the sea) broadly: figurative language—compare, SIMILE. 2. An object or idea.... [13]

I have often thought that what my patients have most wanted from me as they have made their way along the art therapy pilgrimage is an assurance that the truths about their lives are acceptable. In order to fully understand this notion it is of course essential to examine the concept of truth. In the rock opera, *Jesus Christ Superstar,* [14] Caiaphas sings/screams to Jesus, "But what is truth, is truth unchanging law? We both have truths, are mine the same as yours?" It is this question, are my truths the same as yours, that lies at the root of many disturbed persons emotional and psychological dis-ease.

For our purposes here let us define truth as: sincerity in character and action; the sum of real things and events.

The great majority of the patients I have treated, whether in the psychiatric hospital or in my private practice, have suffered from the existential actuality that the truths about their lives have been at best dysfunctional, and at worst horrific. In response to the cognitive and emotional dissonance this causes they have created fictional identities in order to ease the pain. These fictions are of course creative acts in and of themselves, and so are metaphoric portraits of the self, i.e., truths in their own rights.

It is the task of the art therapist to listen to (to see) and share stories through action. Through the doing of art we work with, play with, and enact the salient themes of the therapeutic journey. The critical responsibility is to see and respond to the truths that emerge through the sharing of artistic imagery. We barely need to talk at all. This is risky business for it is of the utmost importance that the visual candors be those of the client, not the therapist. How can this be assured?

Essential to the healing capacity of the art therapist is the use of metaphor. The metaphors of the art therapist are not of the spoken variety. They are figurative actions and objects in which one thing (the patient) is described in the terms of another (the image). The visual metaphors of art therapy hold in tension the potential for multiple interpretations; their purpose being to illuminate or expose the truth.

By our very nature we art therapists are metaphoreticians. It is our task to interact with the graphic symbolic language and actions of our patients. By doing so we translate the myth/metaphor of our patients into token and action within the individual psychotherapy milieu. This is what rituals have done within religious communities for centuries.

The rituals I engage in as an art therapist are the sacraments of the creative process. The preparation of the art studio, the gathering of materials, and the arranging of tables, chairs and easels are the initial actions of the rites that move from within the heart and soul of the patient through the brush and onto the canvas. The themes of these ceremonial pursuits emerge as the intense inward journey of the patient unfolds. As I stand before my patient's canvas I am reverent, awed by the courage so often manifest as the truths and fictions of their lives are portrayed.

I believe that drawings, paintings and sculptures are not mere ideas, they are depictions of life, illustrations of reality. Each jagged line, every vivid form, every chiseled crevice proclaim to the audience (and to the world): *I am here, this is the truth about me!*

Every time my patient scrawls the brilliant red chalk across the page, every time she dips her brush in tempera and moves from palette to canvas she announces to me, "I AM." As I fathom these proclamations I gently seek dialogue. I listen to the whole of the communication and at every turn resist the seductive pull to analyze, dissect and label.

My openness to the artistic work of the patient promotes an atmosphere of contagious excitement regarding self exploration and revelation. As the patient paints or draws in my presence I am keenly attentive to my relationship to her art. I believe that my response to her efforts has tremendous impact, for good or ill, upon the therapeutic journey. It is also essential that I be actively engaged in my own artistic process during these times. My willingness to tell my tale through imagery in the company of the patient sets the stage for the sharing of truths and metaphoric fictions that is the foundation of all therapeutic endeavors.

I must emphasize here that I believe it is imperative to engage in art processes in the course of the therapeutic encounter with the patient. This is a vital element of art therapy practice, not only pragmatically, but ethically imperative. The courage that I honor as I struggle with my own imagery is infectious. It establishes a safe milieu in which the patient is enabled to enter upon his own excursion into self-exploration. As his journey begins, his expressions trickle, ooze, gush, spew and surge onto the page. It is my willingness to be with my own images that lays the groundwork that allows the patient to believe that I will understand his symbolic metaphors. If I can open myself to what he has expressed, the patient feels the twin edges of enjoyment: the vent of emotion for himself, and the awareness that he has been understood by another.

The Gargoyle and Estelle

As I was writing in a patient's medical chart early one morning a nurse placed a piece of folded-up lined notebook paper on the table in front of me. "Look at this!" she said. "This is a really sick one."

I unfolded the paper and beheld a grotesque portrait of a human figure. Although the image was rather disturbing and malevolent in appearance I could see that the artist possessed better than average skills. Drawn with pencil, the line character, use of shading techniques and attention to detail were all quite well done.

The R. N. explained that the drawing had been in the coat pocket of a girl who had been an emergency admission to the adolescent unit the night before. She went on to say that the patient, Estelle, had caused quite a commotion when she was brought in. She had apparently been combative and self-destructive, having bitten her own wrist severely, and required the use of restraints for much of the night. The nurse added that she had howled for several hours, disturbing everyone's sleep.

"So what do you make of this?" She asked.

"Well, it's a little hard to look at, but she does have a good touch with the pencil." I said. "I'll look forward to meeting her when she's ready to be out on the unit or in activities."

"That may be awhile," the nurse muttered. Her tone of voice told me that she found the drawing to be disgusting, pathological and threatening to the security and predictability of the cottage environment.

(This brief interaction illustrates a core tension that often exists between art therapists and members of verbally oriented medical disciplines. While it is the role of the art therapist to value and honor the artistic expressions of patients, no

matter how primitive or disturbing, it is the role of nursing personnel to "keep things on the living unit under control." While I found Estelle's images both grotesque and intriguing, my R. N. colleague saw them as potentially disruptive to the unit. It requires very mature interactive skills, as an art therapist, to travel through the turbulent waters of the psychiatric milieu without offending the boat keepers, nor disturbing the sharks.

A few days passed. I was walking through the unit one afternoon when my attention was caught by a small, frail looking young girl sitting at one of the large round tables in the cafeteria area. She was bent over a sketch pad, working intently. I approached.

"Hello, my name is Bruce."

She did not lift her eyes from the page but said, "Are you the art guy they told me about?

I was surprised, "Yes, how did you know that?

She continued to draw intently. "Some of the other girls were telling me about the adolescent art studio. They described you pretty good. Besides, you are the only guy with a gray beard and no suit and tie."

"You are very observant," I said. "That's a good skill to have if you like art."

"I love art. If I don't die, I might want to be an artist."

"Do you mind if I look at what you are drawing?" I asked.

She did not answer, but pushed the sketch pad across the table toward me. The image was of a nude woman spiked to the ground. Several man/beasts hovered around the woman, holding their genitals in a suggestive manner. The image was provocatively sadistic, yet not without its aesthetic value. I sensed that the girl was tensing up as she watched me look at her work, perhaps expecting that I would be repulsed, or respond in a punitive way. I did neither.

I commented. "You know, the torso of this woman seems a bit out of proportion. Either it is too small, or the head is too large. Did you mean to distort the figure?"

"I wanted the head to be big, because of all the stuff that goes on in my head."

"In that case, you've really done a nice job of presenting a painful and troubling idea. By the way, as I said, my name is Bruce. Who are you?"

For the first time she looked up at me through the strands of hair that fell across her eyes. "I'm Estelle."

I sat down in the chair across the table from her. "It's nice to meet you, Estelle."

She half smiled. "It's nice to have somebody look at my drawings without cringing."

"What do you mean?"

She stared at her hands, then said, "The staff say that I have to close my sketch book whenever any other kids come around. An' I can tell they don't like my drawings."

I thought for a moment, then replied. "You've got good skills. Do you always work in pencil?"

"Yeah," she said. "That's all I ever had at home."

"How about at school?"

"Na, I've been in S. B. H. (severe behaviorally handicapped) since third grade and they didn't have art classes."

"How did you develop your techniques then?"

Estelle offered a wry half smile. "There is a Michaelangelo book in the library at home. I'd check it out and try to copy. I bet I've had that book out a hundred times."

"Well Estelle, I have to get to a meeting. I hope that you'll get out to the studio for adolescent art soon. I'd love to teach you to paint." She said nothing, but as I walked toward the front door of the cottage I could feel her eyes on my back.

A few days later I was told that Estelle would be joining the morning adolescent studio art session. Her treatment team consult form stated that her goals for the studio art experience would be to: 1) Develop a more positive self view through mastery of task. 2) Expand expressive skills, both graphic and verbal. 3) Promote therapeutic alliance through shared task involvements.

She stood in the doorway of the studio, arms folded tightly across her chest, head down, hair falling in an unkempt mane over her eyes. The psychiatric technician who had escorted her to the creative arts building said, "Mr. Moon, this is Estelle. This is her first day off the unit." He whispered to me, "Do you want me to stay here with her, she is a wild one!"

I shook my head. "No, Frank, that won't be necessary. I've met Estelle before, I think things will be ok." I turned to her, "Do you remember me Estelle? I met you the other day on the unit. You showed me one of your drawings.

She half-looked up and said, "You changed your clothes." Then her eyes began to take in the studio.

My colleagues and I try to have as much art as we can hanging on the walls. We hope to create an environment that is stimulating to the creative urge of our patients. We hang current patient works, some of our own paintings and drawings and an occasional piece that's been left behind by former patients. The effect is mildly chaotic, resourceful and contagious. At times the space may appear cluttered and messy but we believe that this sets the tone for the creative process, in that it is also in a constant state of reorganization and structuring. In a wonderful sense the studio is an inanimate symbol of the role of the arts in therapeutic work, i.e., the endless process of making sense out of chaos, order from disorder.

"Estelle," I said, "let me give you a tour of the building." She followed me as I walked her through the various rooms and areas of the creative arts building. As we reentered the studio I asked Estelle if she had any idea of what she'd like to work on.

She shrugged and asked, "Could I use some of that big paper with those drawing pencils you showed me?"

"Sure." I helped her gather the materials she'd asked for: 24″ × 28″ drawing paper, and a set of pencils with varying hardnesses. She chose to work at a table nearest to one of the corners and she sat with her back to the corner so that she could see all that was in the room around her. As she settled in I asked, "Do you have any ideas about what you are going to draw? We like to have people working on themes that are important to them here in the studio."

"I'm going to draw what I always draw, the man."

"All right," I said. "I'll be over here working on my painting. Let me know if you need anything. Welcome to the studio, Estelle."

Saying no more she began to work immediately. Although I worked on my own painting I paid close attention to her progress. Estelle's style of working was unlike any that I'd encountered. She began by drawing one gnarled and spiky hand. She did not sketch the whole figure, nor even the entire hand. Rather, she worked meticulously, one detail at a time. She rendered the thumb, then moved to the index finger, then the middle finger and on to the ring finger, etc. In each instance she completed her drawing of the appendage entirely. Great care and attention was given to the wrinkles of the hand, the crevices and contours, the shadows and highlights. It was as if she could see the finished drawing in its fullness in her mind's eye. It was as if she was a stenographer taking dictation from some unseen imaginal source.

By the end of her first session she had completed one hand, wrist and half of the forearm. In the sessions that followed she continued to work earnestly on her drawing. She seldom spoke to any of her peers in the studio. She routinely made contact with me as she entered the studio, by asking where the pencils were kept. It was obvious that she knew where they were, but that this ritual served as her transition into the creative space. It became the subject of playful cajoling among other adolescents and me. One would ask where the paint brushes were, another would ask where the paper towels were. If Estelle noticed these caricatures enacted around her, she failed to respond in any behavioral manner. I suspect that she was well aware of them and derived some sense of acceptance and pleasure as her peers imitated her interactions with me. It was my hunch that Estelle had often been the brunt of teasing and putdowns in her life. To have her peers impersonate her in a warm spirited manner must have been a delightful change. Had I sensed the slightest quality of brutality in the mimicry I would have put a stop to it immediately. This however had a different gestalt. It was as if Estelle's peers stumbled upon a way to relate to her which she was willing to tolerate.

As the days passed the figure of a grotesque man emerged on the page. Portrayed in harsh light, his muscles rippled, his distorted face cast deep shadows across his beastly hairy chest. It was, to say the least, a frightful and discomforting visage.

As she finished the right wrist she gestured to me, beckoning me to her place in the room. As I approached she said, "Something is wrong." She looked furtively toward her gargoyle.

"What do you mean?" I asked.

She clapped her hand to her face and shook her head. "I can't see what is in the hand."

"Oh, I know that feeling," I said. "Sometimes I feel like the whole canvas is staring at me just waiting for me to do something, only I can't figure out what it is I supposed to do."

"But this never happens to me, Bruce!"

"Estelle, it happens to every artist. You can either try to fight your way through it, or you can just sit back and wait awhile. Either way, something always comes."

She took her hand away from her face. "Do you really believe that?"

"I have a lot of faith in the creative process." I said. "I have learned to trust it."

"How could I fight through this?" She wanted to know.

"Well, one way is to do some study sketches, try out different options. Another way is to ask other people what they think should come next?"

She seemed interested in the latter idea. "Do you ever get ideas that you use from other people?"

"Sure," I said. "And sometimes their ideas spark new ones of my own. It's really just a way to get a different perspective on my work."

She pulled her hair away from her eyes. "So what would you put in the right hand?"

"Hmmm. I think I see a rock, like a rough and jagged piece of quartz or something like that."

She frowned. "I don't know."

"Well, Estelle. There are other people in the room that you could ask."

She turned toward a boy who was working at the next table and asked. "Tony, what do you think should be in my man's right hand?"

He stood up in order to get a better look at the drawing. "I don't know. If it was me I'd probably want it to hold a bag of weed."

Estelle looked over at me as if to say, "what a stupid idea this was, Bruce."

"Try again." I prodded.

"Hanna, what do you think I should add to this drawing?"

Hanna came over and stood behind Estelle. "He sort of reminds me of that guy on *Beauty and the Beast*. Why don't you put yourself in the picture holding hands with the monster?"

A stunned look came over Estelle's face. She did not respond.

"Did I say something wrong? Hanna asked. "I didn't mean to. . . . "

"It's ok, Hanna." I assured her. "Why don't you go back to your work."

Estelle said no more for the rest of that session. In mechanical fashion she cleaned up, put her drawing away and left the building at the end of the period. The following day was a Friday, she refused to attend the session. The next Monday she had a family therapy appointment that conflicted with her studio time so I did not see her until the Tuesday after the events above.

She entered the room. "Where are my pencils?"

"Hi Estelle. They are over on the counter in the white basket."

"I brought some drawings with me for you to look at, Bruce." She laid her sketch book on the table beside my easel. There were three drawings inside the book. The first portrayed a very small child, a toddler, clasping the little finger of the right hand of the gargoyle. The second showed an older child with a balled up fist resting in the open palm of the man. The third appeared to be a detailed self portrait with Estelle's hand depicted gingerly holding the wrist of the right arm, the palm of the hand is again open but appears to be bleeding.

"Yowsa," I exclaimed. "These are not what I expected to see."

"They are what I see." Estelle said quietly.

"Which one are you going to use for your drawing?

"I'm going to use them all," she replied.

"How do you mean," I asked.

"I'm going to do three drawings altogether. This one is for the baby."

Estelle proceeded to finish her first large drawing of the gargoyle. She went on to copy the exact pose of the distorted figure twice more, adding the details described earlier. The result is a triptych of the grotesque and the tender.

Having completed these three works she commenced to work on a large piece of illustration board, approximately four feet square. As she stared at the empty panel Hanna (who had become her roommate back on the unit) said, "Why don't you draw him getting a haircut and a shave?" This brought a small round of laughter from others in the area.

Estelle did not laugh. She threw her pencil to the floor and left the room, making her way to the bathroom down the hall. She did not return to the studio during the rest of that session. She refused to attend the next day.

On the afternoon of the day she had refused I happened to be passing through her unit. I saw her sitting alone in the music listening area. I knocked on the glass door, she waved me in. "Estelle, I missed you this morning in studio."

"Yea, I should have come," she sighed. "Hanna jus' pissed me off the other day and I let it get to me."

"I was wondering about that," I said. "I thought maybe people were trying to make the beast into something he is not."

"Exactly!" Estelle said emphatically. "That's what I hate about that fairy tale. In the end the beauty kisses the beast and he turns into some handsome prince. Why couldn't anybody like him just the way he was?"

"Yes, I know what you mean, Estelle. I think a lot of people have trouble accepting things they see as ugly because it reminds them of parts of themselves."

The gargoyle/beast was seen time and again during the two months that Estelle was in the hospital. Over time his features did soften, becoming less grotesque, less frightening. He never became a handsome prince, but I do believe that he was tamed as Estelle's creativity breathed life into his countenance. Parallel to the changes in the gargoyle were similar changes in Estelle. As she domesticated the beast, she gently tamed her own wildness.

Some would argue that Estelle's drawings did nothing more than chronicle the work that she did in other therapeutic arenas. I suggest that the therapy she was able to do in the psychiatrist's and social worker's offices was made possible through the creative metaphoric work that took place in the art studio.

Chapter VII

FUNDAMENTAL PRINCIPLES OF ART THERAPY

I have often been asked by members of my family, or by friends from other vocational walks of life, to define what art therapy is. It does not matter to them when I explain that I have written two books on the subject and am working on this third text. They want to hear, in thirty seconds or less, what it is that I do.

This chapter will not be able to be compressed into thirty seconds. It will however be a distillation of nearly twenty years of clinical, supervisory and educational experience, an attempt to examine in a few pages what I consider to be the fundamental principles of the field.

1. **Meta-Verbal Therapy.** First and foremost is the idea that the essential work of art therapy takes place in the interaction between the patient/artist, the media, the image and the process. In this sense the primary task of the art therapist is to set the stage for the work to unfold. The art therapist need not be a clever manipulator of words intended to interpret and analyze the imaginal efforts of the patient.

This is an easy concept to grasp in relation to work in the fine arts studio. It is somewhat more difficult to understand as a fully expressive psychotherapy group and individual work. When I stress this point to my students they often challenge this tenet. My response is consistent. I believe that the majority of the work that takes place in an expressive art group psychotherapy session has been done before the patient ever says a word about their image. Essentially, talking about the art work is the icing on the cake. The main course of the therapeutic meal takes place between patient, process and product. The substance of the art therapy session is beyond the spoken word. This is not a devaluation of verbalization, it is rather an honoring of action and image. I have participated in many hours of art therapy work where little or nothing was said, but much was done.

2. **Talk as Validation.** Given the position I have adopted above, one may wonder why I (or any art therapist) would ever talk at all? Humans are by nature talkative creatures. Talking about images, paintings or

drawings offers some measure of security for both patient and therapist. For the patient, the act of talking about their artistic processes and products provides an opportunity to distance from the powerful feelings often evoked through the work. As the patient searches for words to describe the enterprise he shifts out of a primarily sensual and emotional position, toward an acceptable cognitive construct. In some cases this may be quite helpful to the patient. In other instances it may be problematic. For example:

In the case of a young woman suffering a severe anxiety disorder, with features of Post Traumatic Stress Disorder, it was most helpful to encourage her to speak of the pictures of the horrors of the sexual abuse she had endured at the hands of her uncle. It was soothing to her to be assured by the therapist and her peers in the group that little children are in no position to ward off such inappropriate sexual behaviors on the part of adult authority figures. The group put it into words this way, "It wasn't your fault, Sarah, you are guilty of nothing. You have a right to be angry at him, but you should no longer be ashamed." In this instance the words offered the patient comfort and consolation as she wrestled with the demons of her history.

In contrast is the case of the mid-forties salesman who came to the hospital, seeking treatment for his depression. It became clear very quickly that in addition to being depressed, he was drinking excessively and was probably an alcoholic. He was a charming, yet subtly untrustworthy man. He was quite adept at using his words to keep himself a safe distance from those around him, while at the same time seeming to be the life of the party.

In response to the drawing task, "Portray the animal in your head and the animal in your gut," he drew a collie dog for the head, and a hideous dragon in his belly. As it came his turn to share in the group about his drawing he launched into a lengthy, entertaining monologue. He had everyone in the room laughing heartily at his story. I said nothing. As his story wound down I was able to establish eye contact with him. Without speaking I shook my head slowly, side to side. The group, sensing an unspoken tension, quieted.

He looked at me. "What?"

I opened my mouth, as if about to speak, but remained silent.

He raised his voice. "What's your problem?"

Intuiting that any effort I made to interact with him through talking would be an exercise in futility, I raised my right hand, gesturing toward the image of the collie. I mimed petting the dog gently. With my left hand I reached trembling toward the dragon. As one hand amiably stroked the air, the other shook with growing intensity. I looked from hand to hand, then to the patient.

His face reddened. "What is that bullshit all about?" He pointed toward my hands. "Is that supposed to mean something?"

I gently nodded my head affirmatively.

He snorted, "This is a bunch of shit. I don't get it, I don't get any of it."

I quietly said, "I believe you."

Looking toward his peers with mixed annoyance and desperation he jeered, "I'm lost, man."

Again I said, "I believe you."

"What the hell are you talking about?"

"I believe you. I believe that you feel lost."

In this illustration words were used sparingly and only in an effort to verify the deep meanings expressed in the images of the patient. I felt very little pull to talk during this interchange. It was apparent that, at a preverbal level, the patient had already begun to struggle with the issues of his tame and charming exterior and his wild and repugnant inner feelings as characterized in the animal imagery. There was little need to talk.

I want to be completely clear regarding this point: The essential role of verbalization in art therapy must be regarded as one of confirmation. The crucial work in the art therapy session takes place between the artist/patient, the media, and their image in the presence of the art therapist.

3. **Art Therapy Has No Discriminatory Borders.** It can be used with the very young through the very old. No one is disqualified on the basis of gender or sexual orientation. Just as the arts themselves are multi-cultural, so too, art therapists work with persons from all races, creeds and religious traditions. Art therapy is effective with individuals, couples, families and groups. It works well with the intellectually gifted and the learning impaired. It can be used with the chronically mentally ill, the terminally ill, the vision impaired and the deaf.

Throughout human history wherever people have gathered together to form communities, the arts have sprung to life. Similarly, wherever suffering persons gather seeking help, the arts emerge as a potent psychic balm.

4. **The Dynamic Energy Generated Through Creative Action is of Conse-**

quential Merit as a Source of Satisfaction and Validation of Personal Worth.

I am repeatedly awed by the look in my patients' eyes as they sign their work, stand back and gaze at what they have done. The air in the room is filled with the soundless proclamations by the artist, I AM!

5. **Artistic Expression is a Healthy Act.** Don Jones, A. T. R., H. L. M., one of the pioneers of the art therapy profession, repeatedly emphasized in his teaching, "You must treat the dysfunction of the patient by functioning with the patient."

A simplified illustration of Don's point is found in the case of a severely depressed man who, prior to coming to the hospital had retreated to his bed and refused all of his normal life responsibilities. While the resident psychiatrist assigned to treat the man was captivated by his explanations of his disease, Don's approach was to insist that the patient be expected to participate in the morning physical conditioning activity in the hospital gym. This was followed by an hour in the creative arts studio. Not surprisingly the patient reported feeling noticeably better by the afternoon of the second day that he participated in the calisthenics and painting group. It feels good to do. It particularly feels good to express yourself artistically.

6. **Treatment, Whether Psychological or Rehabilitative, is Stimulated and Enhanced Through the Use of Imagination.** Often, before the patient can fully put things into words, issues arise and are worked with through engagement with imagery and fantasy.

A Penny For Your Thoughts

Penny's depression was profound and baffling. Her father reported that prior to that year she had always been an outgoing and cheerful girl. She'd gotten good grades, been a cheerleader, and was a popular and active kid. In fact, he said that since her mother had died of cancer three years earlier, she had "been a real trooper." Penny had taken over caring for her younger brother and sister. She cleaned the house, cooked the meals and organized the family's life as best she could. Over the summer she had become gradually less active. As school began in the fall Penny withdrew from her extracurricular activities. The first grading period yielded a marked drop in her grades. Finally, late one Saturday evening, her father found her slumped in a chair in her bedroom. He tried to awaken her but she failed to respond. He immediately called the rescue squad and she was taken to a local hospital where her stomach was pumped. She had taken a handful of sleeping pills.

During the first few days of her hospitalization, Penny was listless. Although she cooperated with the treatment program, she did so in a passive manner, as if she were just going through the motions. She didn't talk much, to anyone.

However, her initial drawing in expressive art psychotherapy group spoke volumes. The task that I had assigned that day was to "Imagine that you've been walking in the woods. You come upon the mouth of a cave. For a moment you consider walking past, but your curiosity won't allow it. I want you to pretend that you go into the cave, to the deepest part. Look around yourself, what do you see? How does it smell, how does it feel in there?"

Penny's image was of a large Winnie-the-Pooh-like bear standing in front of the cave opening. The mouth of the cave was dark and foreboding behind the bear. A tiny child was portrayed standing before the bear.

When it was her turn to share about her drawing she said, "I couldn't get into the cave. The bear wouldn't get out of my way!"

"It looks like a very big bear." I responded.

"Yes," Penny said. "He is big. He wasn't mean or anything like that, but he wouldn't move."

"This is a really interesting picture, Penny. Would you be willing to use your imagination and talk with me about it?"

She nodded her head.

"Good," I said. "Now what I'd like for you to do, Penny, is pretend that you are Winnie the Pooh and that you can talk. I'll be the girl in the picture. What would you say to me?"

She closed her eyes momentarily. "I'd say, get out of here. This is no place for little girls."

"But I want to go in there and look around," I replied.

In a slightly more stern voice Penny said, "Go home to your mother. This cave is dark and wet and scary. You don't want to go in there."

"Oh but I do," I said. "I want to explore."

The bear growled. "You have no business in there. If you go in you may never come out again. Now go home to your mother like I told you to." As these words left her lips Penny began to weep. She would say no more during that session.

The ensuing weeks of treatment explained the significance of this first drawing. The portrait of Pooh and Penny and the Cave captured the essence of her therapeutic journey.

The cave represented Penny's developmental need to separate herself from her family. The crucial task of adolescence is the work of emancipation. Her mother's death had interrupted her process of separation and individuation. Perhaps the cave symbolized her need to experiment with sexuality. It may have symbolized her struggle to understand her own interior depths. It certainly allegorized the adolescent psychic tasks of self-exploration.

The Pooh bear stood in her way, representing the obstacles in her emancipation path. Among these were her father, her younger siblings, and the absence of her mother. The message of the bear was plain, "Don't explore the dark and wet regions of yourself. In effect, "Don't grow up."

Significant in the imaginal dialogue between Penny and the bear (Penny and herself) were the repeated references that the bear made to, "Go home to your mother." The message was that the only way past the obstacles to emancipation was to join the mother, i.e., kill yourself.

At another level this drawing revealed the guilt that Penny felt. The guilt stemmed from her preconscious sense that she had won the *Oedipal* battle. Mother was dead and she was now in the position of wife to her father. Compounding the guilt were her feelings regarding her own longing for sexual contact with peers, anger at having been thrust into an adult role too early in her life, and resentment of her younger siblings.

Penny was not in the hospital very long. The drawing provided the treatment team with the keys to understanding her suicidal attempt and the underlying feelings. Once these were understood it was relatively easy to begin to counter her unrealistic guilt with supportive reassurance that her feelings were natural. Family therapy helped to lighten the expectations on Penny; roles within the family unit were redefined, making the everyday tasks much less burdensome.

Penny's psychotherapy was defined by the images she created in the expressive art psychotherapy group.

7. The Therapeutic Use of Art Provides an Opportunity for the Patient-Artist to Render Emotional Portraits of Significant Others in Their Lives.

The poignancy of this principle was illustrated for me early in my career as I treated a woman named Helen. She entered the hospital in the midst of a profound depression. Her husband had died unexpectedly a few months earlier. Since his death she had gradually become less active, and withdrawn from her family and friends. Ultimately, she had ceased to function, choosing to isolate herself at home, doing nothing.

The attending psychiatrist's hypothesis was that there were many unresolved issues between Helen and her late husband and that these blocked her ability to grieve. The problem for the treatment team then was how to engage a dead man in the therapy work that Helen needed to do?

The answer that emerged was that Helen would be encouraged to draw and paint images of her husband and their relationship. One such drawing portrayed Helen discovering the fallen body in their kitchen. As she finished the image I saw that tears were welling up in her eyes. When she began to speak of this drawing, however, the feelings connected to it were not sadness or loss. Helen was angry. Something about the way that she portrayed the scene had sparked the anger she felt toward her husband for deserting her.

Raising her voice she addressed the picture, "How could you leave me here all alone? We were supposed to retire together, see the world and live happily ever after. How dare you ruin everything!"

As her words hung in the air she began to cry.

In later drawings Helen was able to dialogue with her husband. She imagined what he would say to her. Through this process she was able to resolve symbolically some of her feelings abandonment, loss, and anger.

8. **The Creative Arts Provide Opportunities to Make Concrete Objects Representing Feelings and Thoughts That are Elusive, Hidden and Mysterious.** This affords both the therapist and the patient a *thing* to dialogue about and with. Patients often experience talking about the characters in their images as less threatening than discussing their psychological difficulties directly.

It is a safe assumption that patients admitted to psychiatric hospitals have already tried to alleviate their emotional distress on an outpatient basis. This means that they have tried traditional verbal psychotherapy without significant relief. The same holds true for the individual who seeks art therapy on an outpatient basis; i.e., they have usually engaged in other forms of therapy to no avail. The reasons for the failure of verbal psychotherapy are, of course, as numerous and varied as the patients themselves.

It is the creation of an objective thing that separates art therapy from the work done by psychologists, social workers, psychiatrists and counselors. The painting, the sculpture, the drawing, is the focal object. It is through the creation of the thing that the relationship between art therapist and patient is constructed. The object provides both a subject and context for being together. Sometimes the work is spoken about. Sometimes the patient is asked to give the image a voice and to speak from its perspective. Other times there is no talking at all.

Rob's World

I first met Rob when he was referred to the art studio. The instructions of the treatment team were to help Rob develop expressive skills. He was a hostile and rather crude young man, twenty-five years old. He'd been admitted to the hospital upon the recommendation of his lawyer. He was facing serious charges of assault and battery and the lawyer felt that evaluation of his mental health might be beneficial to his defense.

Rob was a big guy, 6′ 4″ tall, weighing 225 lbs. He was not pleased about being in the hospital, despite the fact that he had signed a voluntary admission agreement. Within a few short hours in the hospital he had established his pattern of relating. He intimidated peers and staff members. He was loud and vulgar.

He came to the arts studio on his second day of hospitalization. He'd been in the building for only a few minutes when his obnoxious verbal devaluing began.

He raised his voice. "This is ridiculous. Why in the hell do you want me play around with this bull?"

"Rob," I said. "I know that doing art is often something that people have not done for a long time when they come in here. But, we think that it is a very healthy thing to do, and it might help us understand you a little better." It was my sense that Rob's bravado was a cover for serious feelings of inadequacy and self-loathing. The volume level of his resistance seemed almost desperate, as if demanding attention and care.

He snarled, "So, wha'd'ya want me to do?" I handed him a piece of masonite, approximately 18″ × 24″ in size.

"I'd like you to think about a rock.

"Why should I think about a rock?"

"Well, you seem to be a really strong and solid guy," I said. "Maybe if you painted a picture of a rock it might help me understand how you feel."

Rob replied, "I ain't got any feelings!"

I said, "Do you mean that you are numb . . . or empty . . . or dead?"

"Huh?"

"Rob, in order to have no feelings at all you either have to be numb, empty or dead. Which are you?

He slammed his meaty fist on the table. "I ain't none of that."

"Alright Rob. Let's back up. What kind of rock shall we paint?"

He thought for a few moments. "Coal!"

"OK," I said. "I'd like you to begin by painting this masonite like fire."

He gave me a puzzled glance. "Why fire?"

"You seem pretty angry about things Rob, so I thought of fire when you said coal."

"So how do I start? I don't know how to make no fire."

I suggested that he place several blobs of orange, yellow and red paint randomly on the masonite. When he had done so I showed him how to use a large brush in continuous long strokes to pull the paint across the board. I could tell that he was immediately gratified when the warm colors blended together as he drew the brush from left to right.

"Damn, this is all right." He exclaimed.

The next day I asked Rob to imagine the shape of the coal that he wanted to paint.

He said, "I dunno. Jus' coal shaped."

"Well, how about taking a piece of notebook paper and crumpling it up so it's shaped like a rock?"

Rob told me he'd try.

A few minutes later he brought me a wadded piece of paper. I said, "Good job, Rob. It really looks like a piece of coal. Now try to draw it onto the board with a piece of chalk." When he had finished that task I again praised his effort.

"Now what," he asked.

I replied. "Now I want you to paint it pure black."

When he completed that he said that he thought there should be some, "lines or something," to show the shape of the coal. I suggested that he use blue to indicate the edges and surfaces of the piece of coal.

When Rob finished his painting he received a number of positive comments from his peers in the studio. He seemed genuinely surprised and pleased by their praise. It happened that he was the last of the patients to leave the creative arts building that morning. I was at the sink cleaning some paint brushes.

"Ya know, I never did paint anything before in my life, 'cept the garage."

I looked up from the sink, "You did well, Rob. I like the image a lot."

"I wanted to ask you something," he said.

"Ask away."

"I know that this sounds funny, but when I look at that thing I uh . . . uh . . . "

"It makes you feel something?"

"Yeah, isn't that screwy?"

I dried my hands. "It happens all the time, Rob. I think that pictures sometimes know more about us than we do."

"What?" He looked at me incredulously.

"Never mind," I said. "I wonder what that piece of coal would say if it had a voice?"

Rob laughed, then feigned a tortured scream.

"That doesn't sound angry." I said.

"It ain't angry. It's bein' burned up, that would hurt!"

This was the first small hint that Rob gave us that there was more to him than the angry, macho facade he showed the world. Other paintings and sculptures followed. Images of his loneliness, self loathing and inadequacies emerged from this rough and vulgar young man. He seldom talked at length about his works. They spoke for him eloquently. In rare moments Rob was able to put words to his art. However, when it was suggested directly that perhaps the feelings he associated with his pictures might be his own, he quickly retreated into his brutish style of interaction. As long as the image was the subject of conversation he would try to stay with it. As soon as Rob himself became the focus his bravado and ignobility returned. Through his images Rob was able to share his feelings of emptiness, anger and sadness. These aspects of self would never have been known had it not been for his objects of art.

9. **The Primary Feelings Related to Events in the Patient's Life Remain Powerfully Attached to Artistic Portrayals.** All artists can attest to this fact. As a drawing is done representing an incident, regardless of how long ago, the feelings of that event are recalled with much the same power that they held at their occurrence.

Every so often I rearrange the storage space in my studio. As I do, I am bombarded by the image memories held in the paintings and drawings that I am relocating. Each work contains an emotional charge. At one level I can recall the sensations of the scene. I smell the smells and hear the sounds. At another level I can also recall the process of creating the work. I remember the period of my life that produced the piece, the pleasures and the struggles.

The technical psychological term for this process is cathexis, i.e., *investment of libidinal energy in a person, object, or idea.*

As an art therapist I have seen this phenomenon time and again as patients portray painful experiences from their childhood. In the context of the art therapy session it is as if the art therapist and patient enter a time machine and are transported back to the traumatic event. This provides both with a window to the past. This is a particularly important characteristic of the therapeutic use of the arts, for often patients experience extreme difficulty relating to the distant past through verbal constructions. This is why art therapy has become one of the primary treatment modalities for persons suffering from post traumatic stress disorder. P. T. S. D. patients, whether suffering from the after effects of war, physical, sexual or emotional abuse, come to treatment longing to reclaim their own tragic past in order to live peacefully with their present. Images which remain cathected to traumatic events are the key to understanding the experiences of the patient. Likewise, the cathartic process of artistic expression offers the P. T. S. D. patient an opportunity to purge destructive emotions and bring about spiritual renewal which is integral to their recovery.

10. **As Art Therapists We Have Two Essential Tools, ART, and OUR-SELVES.** The essential nature of the arts processes have been, and will be, explored throughout this book. The use of ourselves as a therapeutic tool is a vital concept. It is critical that we art therapists know ourselves well before we attempt to deal with the lives of others. We cannot afford to have emotional blind spots which obscure our vision of the patient. We must know ourselves well, and whenever possible we must be at peace in our own being. I do not see how it is possible to be an effective therapist when your own life is in extreme turmoil.

I do not intend to suggest that an art therapist should withdraw from the field at times of great personal stress. Rather, I suggest that we must all be willing to work on ourselves. This means that at times in one's professional life there will be occasions when personal psychotherapy will be of great help. Being an art therapist is not a normal existence. Becoming an art therapist requires an extraordinary capacity to introspect and struggle with the images that emerge in one's own art works. We should not be shy about seeking therapy, for this is an investment, not only in our own well being, but in the well being of our patients as well.

We must be willing to grapple with our own motivations, fantasies and desires which led us to this profession. This means coming face to face with our strengths, weaknesses, virtues and evils. We must wrestle with our omnipotent longings as they bump against our impotent realities. We must realize that as art therapists we are only catalysts for change in the patient's life. We cannot make someone be healthy, for that is their responsibility.

I encourage all students and colleagues to consider entering psycho-therapy. Ideally this can do no harm, and has the potential to do much good. As the proverb instructs, *Physician, heal thyself,* I urge art therapists to know themselves well.

Chapter VIII

TO TALK, OR NOT TO TALK

There is no more troubling question for the arts therapy profession than *what is the role of talking?* How much should I say? When should I say it? What should I say? Do I need to say anything at all? What if I can't think of anything to say?

As art therapists we exist in the world of medical professions, allied health professions, and educational professions. Each of these disciplines depend utterly upon the written and spoken word. Yet we, by our nature often find ourselves dealing with that which cannot be sensibly put into words. We operate in a world of images, colors, shadows, sensations and intuitions.

It its beginnings psychotherapy was termed, "the talking cure." What is our place in the realm of the psychiatrist, psychologist, social worker and nurse, all of whom use verbalization as their primary mode of interaction?

Words and Pictures From the Border

In the winter of 1984 Dr. Carol Lebeiko, a child psychiatrist and I began working as co-therapists in an expressive art psychotherapy group. The collaboration that we began a decade ago continues to the time of this writing. The uniqueness of our joint venture lies in our ability to honor each other's disciplinary gifts. Carol brings her tradition of verbal psychotherapy. I bring my respect for the unspoken power of images.

The patients that we selected for involvement in our first group were highly verbal, skillfully defended, manipulative and powerful border-line personality adolescent girls. Beyond the age, sex and diagnostic criteria for entry into the group, we also sought those patients who seemed to be slipping through the cracks in the hospital's therapeutic foundation. They were gliding through treatment as though coated in Teflon. No therapeutic interventions or interpretations were getting beyond their pathological armor. Their verbal therapists were stuck.

Rachel's Tears

Rachel entered the group after having been in the hospital for nearly a month. She was a pretty, intelligent, outwardly cheerful sixteen year old. She had, prior to coming into the group, remained distant and unattached to the treatment staff. She'd been hospitalized several times before coming to Harding. Her primary difficulties were identified as alcohol and drug abuse, intense enmeshment with mother, sexual promiscuity and teen-aged motherhood. In addition she had exhibited antisocial behaviors including vandalism, theft and assaultive behaviors. Criminal charges were pending in two states. It was also of diagnostic interest that Rachel's mother had adopted Rachel's baby, further complicating and cementing their intense conflictual relationship.

Her primary modes of relating to the treatment staff and her peers were two-fold. She alternated between a coy, child-like superficiality and a pseudo-mature seductive style. Both served her well in keeping others at a safe distance from any genuine relationship with her.

On her first day in the expressive art psychotherapy group the chasm between her outward demeanor and her inner sense of self became blatantly apparent. As we went through the beginning ritual of sitting in a circle and checking in with each group member Rachel commented, "I'm just great," and she flashed a pearly smile around the circle.

When everyone had their turn I suggested that the drawing topic for that session was to, "draw how you really feel." Rachel quickly gathered red and black chalk and drew a slashing, spinning symbol on her 3′ × 3′ piece of brown paper. As the group sat down to share their images I joked about Rachel's drawing, "Wow, that sure looks great!" She smiled.

Dr. Lebeiko asked Rachel if she would give her drawing a voice. "What would it say, Rachel?"

Rachel's smile disappeared momentarily but she remained silent.

I asked the group, "As you listen to this image, what do you hear?"

One girl said, "I hear I'm angry."

Another said, "Hurt."

Another, "I'm lonely."

Rachel blurted out, "Ok, ok, so I feel like shit, so what?"

Carol quickly voiced the message of how important it was to have a place to express how we *really* feel. Rachel teared up, but she was not about to let anyone see her cry. The smile returned.

Some of Rachel's most significant work in the group took place while I was away from the hospital for a brief period. This was an intensely difficult time for the group members for it reenacted the abandonment themes which lay at the root of the dysfunction for each of them. They seized this opportunity and in a pathological manner acted out all of their hostility toward maternal figures on Carol. This was no picnic for Carol, to endure the attacks of each of these girls; however it was a crucial opportunity to see their illness acted out on the therapeutic stage. Grist for the mill. Rachel was the most vicious of the six as she projected years of rage and frustration. She was covertly elected leader of the resistance movement, by her peers.

When I returned, as I saw each member in passing, there was a gush of, "Oh God, group was so boring . . . stupid . . . waste of time, etc. It was clear that the dynamic of devaluation of the mother, coupled with idealization of the father, was in full swing.

Our warm up drawing in the next session was benignly assigned as, "Catch me up on how life has been in this group." There was a flurry of ventilation on the walls of the expression room. I made no comments as the group members spewed their hostility toward Carol. Nor did I remark on their subtler message, "please make it all better now." After everyone had a chance to vent about what they'd drawn, we moved on to the main theme of the day. The task was to draw a portrait of yourself and someone important to you."

I had anticipated that Rachel would draw either her mother or her baby. What she drew however, was a profound expression of the splitting process that she was so actively engaged in. The drawing portrayed herself looking into a mirror. The mirror reflected an ugly, fat, hateful and lonely image.

As the counterparts, one perfect, one horrible, began to dialogue, Rachel became tearful and vulnerable in the group for the first time. Her peers were at last able to see beyond the polished veneer that she had so skillfully maintained.

The mirror became the dominant visual metaphor for Rachel in the sessions that followed. When she left the hospital I believe that her mirror reflected a genuine image of Rachel, complete with good and bad, beauty and blemish.

The words that were used during her tenure in the group were relatively few. The bulk of her work took place between herself, the paper, the chalk and her images.

Amanda's Rage

When we announced to the group that Amanda would be joining us there was a pronounced silence. Finally, one of the girls shared that she was frightened of Amanda. Amanda had quite a reputation on the adolescent unit. She was a large, masculine appearing girl whose arms bore gruesome testimony to her serious suicidal and self mutilating efforts. She had a way of looking threatening. Her favorite pastime was lifting weights. She didn't like to talk, but she did draw. Having heard so much about her, my fantasy about her involvement in the group was not pleasant. I envisioned resistance, testing of the limits, intimidation and conflict with the other group members. (I have so little faith in the power of art sometimes.)

My fantasy fell apart, however, on Amanda's first week in the group. Where I expected resistance, I found attachment. Where I anticipated limit testing, I found compliance and investment in the process. Where I feared intimidation and conflict, I found a catalyst for meaningful engagement in the group task. It became clear very quickly that Amanda's tough style and appearance was only that, style and appearance.

A poignant illustration of this came on a day that the assigned task was to portray three significant events in your life. Remarkably, everyone's graphics included one reference to death and one symbolic visage of loss.

Amanda's drawing was extremely powerful in its simplicity. There were two tombstones beside a campfire. As Amanda began to share with the group about her images there was a marvelous metamorphosis. The silence and attention in the room was electric. The first tombstone represented the death of a neighbor. "He was really like my father. Like a father ought to be." The second symbolized her grandmother. "She was really my mom. My real mom was never around." The fire represented the warmth and security she felt when she was with these two. "They made me feel like I was somebody. I had a place in their lives."

As another patient talked about what it was like for her when her parents got divorced, Amanda chimed in, "Yeah, when my parents were always fighting I'd just watch from the corner. I knew I didn't belong there."

In that session Amanda metaphorically illustrated the crux of her difficulties. Her experience of anger as the force that kept her from belonging was the dynamic that pushed her to attempt to rigidly control her own rage. Her unfathomable fear of anger stemmed from a deep belief that to be angry would lead to having no sense of acceptance. She used all of her emotional energy to control, to keep herself from exploding. The pressure mounted, she controlled and the pressure continued to build. She perceived herself as a fire breathing dragon. The equation was eminently clear to Amanda. Anger = loss. Yet, she had so much to be angry about. Her only avenue for release was in self-destructive and self-defeating behaviors, i.e. cutting herself. The emotional payoff was that these actions eventually got her the attention she so desperately needed. The pattern had become, "If I tell anyone I'm angry I will be rejected, but if I hurt myself I will get attention and nurturance plus everyone will know that I was angry." It was a great system, crazy perhaps, but it served her well.

The therapeutic task was to provide Amanda with alternative behaviors, nurturance and acceptance like she had experienced with her grand-mother and neighbor. Essentially we wanted to help her learn to explode with color and line on the expressive room walls rather than implode on her arms. While words were a part of the process, they were by no means a major component of the therapeutic work with, and for, Amanda.

Tarri's Castle

Of all our initial patients, Tarri was the most disturbed and disturbing. A moody, intelligent, volatile, bi-racial girl who was capable of being the center-of-attention comedienne who made everyone on the unit laugh. She could also withdraw from the world, acknowledging no one at all. I had seen her, in a fit of rage, pound her fists wildly against her own face.

Tarri had been adopted at age two. She was cute, a fairly light skinned girl with deep brown eyes. Her adoptive parents were blonde, blue eyed people, with two older children of their own.

For the treatment team Tarri was a difficult patient to understand. Her mood shifts were so dramatic at times that some thought she might be an adolescent multiple personality. She complained of hearing voices, some thought she was psychotic. Tarri had no way of describing or sharing her experience of the world. There were no words for her to offer. She was removed, distant, and suspicious of the staff. Nothing the treatment team did seemed to dent her armor.

In the expressive art psychotherapy group she seldom spoke. She responded to questions with yes or no answers. Graphically however, she poured on to the page images of the chaos she felt internally. Her startling pictures were always bound by thick, hard edged containing lines.

In one session I asked the group to portray themselves in some other time and place, either past or future. Tarri drew a complicated scene from medieval days. She cast herself as a fair, helpless maiden who'd been trapped by a dragon. She also depicted a knight, but his armor was rusted and he appeared powerless before the dragon. This drawing symbolized the dilemma of Tarri and each of her peers in the group.

The image of the maiden represented the innocent helplessness, i.e., the child within each of them that had ceased to develop. The dragon encapsulated the rage that held the maiden prisoner. The rusty knight symbolized the futility of hope and their lack of faith in relationship with others.

In a later session Tarri drew her "life as a landscape." She portrayed a nearly barren desert scene. There was a tiny pool near the center of the page. The pool was surrounded by a fence and by a high stone wall. As the group talked about the drawings that day Tarri spoke haltingly of the emptiness and loneliness of her desert. When I asked her about the pool she said, "It's really just a wish."

I responded, "Tarri, I believe that everything we draw is a self portrait." She blandly replied, "Oh."

I asked her to pretend that she was swimming in the pool. Her eyes lit up as she described diving into cool, clear water. She told us that it was a secret place where only she could go. "This is my place."

Carol then led the group in a discussion of how much each member longed for a place that was her own where she could feel safe and secure, knowing that they belonged.

This drawing marked a turning point for Tarri. The pool became a recurrent symbol. In the sessions that followed she talked more openly about her longing for a home. The more she talked, the more it inspired others to share their feelings of abandonment and yearning.

Several weeks later Tarri entered the room in a dismal mood. I tried to ask her what was going on but received a non-response. I asked her to draw what was on her mind. She divided her page in half. On one side she drew a desolate landscape with a small house standing beside a road that led off into the distant nothingness. The other side was filled with a lush garden/jungle scene.

She sat staring at her picture for a few minutes, then quietly said, "I've made up my mind, I can't go back to that house. I don't belong there. I never have." No other words were said. She sat, she cried.

I cannot over emphasize the significance of this drawing. The desolate landscape represented Tarri's adoptive parents' plans and expectations for her. The garden, her own goals. At a deeper level these images presented a portrait of a square peg who had run out of energy trying to fit into a round hole. At times there were words to frame her experience, but often the images simply spoke for themselves.

In our early days of doing co-therapy Carol would occasionally suggest that we spend more time talking in the group in the traditional open ended non-directive style in which she had been trained. This was clearly a more familiar orientation for her. Despite my uneasiness with non-directive approaches, for a time we did abandon the structure of doing art as the focus of the group.

I opened one session by announcing to the group that we had decided to shift gears and just talk about whatever they wished to discuss. The silence in the room was deafening. Forty-five minutes of anxious nothingness followed.

The next session the patients opened by complaining that the group was no longer helping them and that it was boring. Three of them stated that they were going to request to be removed from the group.

After several fruitless sessions I again raised the issue of art structures with Dr. Lebeiko. In looking back on that phase of the group's life there are at least two possible explanations of why so little happened. 1. We had given into the powerful resistance patterns of the patients. When they complained about the artistic processes as tiresome, they were really saying that they were painful, hard work that they wished to avoid. Their drawings inevitably brought them face to face with the struggles of their lives. 2. We had abandoned the non-directive approach too early: i.e., our own anxiety pushed us to become more controlling so that something of value would occur in the sessions.

Both explanations may have some truth. Clearly not much observable work occurred in the group when we tried to rely on verbal, non-directive process. My bias is that it was the drawing process that provided a safe and secure environment in which to struggle metaphorically with the intense conflictual issues of each group member. Powerful feelings just leak out onto the page. Once there they can no longer be dodged or circumvented by defensive verbalization.

Regardless of which explanation is the most valid, we did return to the use of artistic tasks in the structure of the group. Immediately the group was able to refocus on feelings related to the abandonment, self-hatred and rage that each member felt.

At the time of this writing Carol and I have worked together for nearly ten years. We have expanded our groups to include patients of many diagnostic categories. We have included males, and our average length of treatment stay with our patients has dwindled from one year (when we began the group) to slightly more than two weeks. Despite these radical shifts in group composition and duration of treatment the work remains essentially the same. The role of words in the expressive art group psychotherapy process may best be described as one of honoring and validating the artistic expressions of our patients. Nothing less, nothing more. I remain cautious regarding the need to talk.

Chapter IX

CONFLICT

Perhaps the most surprising aspect of the field of art therapy to the novice student is the inherent presence of conflict, in both the academic and clinical environments.

Conflict: *the opposition of persons or forces that gives rise to the dramatic action in a drama or fiction.* [13]

Perhaps this is related to motivations that lead students into the field. I stated in Chapter I that I believe our primary motivation is love. The novice, being drawn to the profession by their longing to be of service to humankind, is often taken aback by the intense oppositional forces they confront as they begin their lives as art therapists. They come to the discipline wearing rose colored glasses, full of good will and best intentions. Very soon, however, they must contend with the ill-tempered patient who defeats their warmest maneuvers, and the professor who demands that they document their papers according to A. P. A. format and is disinterested in the wonderful content of their work. They are confronted with the peer in graduate school who thrives on competition, and who stirs all of their worst fears of inadequacy.

Conflict is everywhere in the world of the art therapist. The patient seeks therapy, not out of harmony and peace, but out of dissonance and emotional combat. There are, even in the best treatment milieus, inter-disciplinary rivalry, philosophic disagreement and political clashes. Even within the art therapy profession itself there have been heated disputes throughout its history.

In order to deal with the presence of conflict I have found it helpful to work toward an understanding of the role of discord in human existence.

Life begins in struggle. The pre-birth hours are filled with hesitant, painful movement away from the safety and warmth of the womb, toward the bright, cold uncertainty of life outside. The birth process is the first conflict in the life of a person. As such it symbolizes much of what is to follow, a life composed of one conflict after another.

Reflect for a moment on a few of the developmental tasks and existential concerns that await the newborn. There are the initial struggles to communicate one's need for food, dryness, warmth, fondling and love, all without the advantage of speech. Then come encounters with the outside world, parents, siblings and peers. The feelings of loss and rejection the first time that the mother leaves the child in the care of another. The first day of kindergarten. The first run-in with the school bully. The first awareness of bodily changes in puberty. The first date. The first rejection. The first move away from home. Marriage. The birth of one's own children, and on and on the conflictual cycle spins. From beginning to end our lives are flooded with inevitable change, and unavoidable conflict.

One of the finer attributes of humanity is our resilience in the face of the instability around us. Our capacity to adapt, to change, and to struggle with conflict, both internal and external, is remarkable. It is a tenet of existentialism that the worth of an individual's existence is determined by how he or she responds to conflict and anguish.

The individual's ability to creatively contend with the skirmishes of his life marks the difference between a productive, authentic existence and a life marked with defeat and emptiness. This capacity may be described as coping skill, defense mechanism, adaptability or optimism. For our purposes here I will call it creative resolution.

Let me turn briefly to my theological tradition in order to describe the foundation of creative resolution. In the Biblical book of Genesis the reader is, in the first sentence, confronted with an image of God as *CREATOR.* "In the beginning God created . . . " Within a few passages we read that God created man in His own image. At this point in the Biblical text the only thing we know of God is that God creates. One may presume, then, that this is one primary characteristic that human beings share with God, we create.

In the modern era the image of people as creative beings has been lost. It is as though creativity is seen as the private attribute of the artist, entertainer or scientist. We seldom speak of the creative potential of *the average Joe* who works on an assembly line. Those who define themselves as creative all too often indulge in a form of elitism, excluding the common person from the ranks of the creative. The severity of such an error is not only that the "creative people" delude themselves, but that frequently the world at large accepts the prejudice.

It hasn't always been this way. Prior to the industrial revolution every man and woman had to utilize their creativity in order to survive. When faced with the realities of making shelter, food, clothing, tools and entertainment, people created or perished. The conflicts were ever present and the capacity for creative resolution determined one's fate.

In this age of mass manufactured housing, processed food, designer clothing and the instant diversion of television our conflicts are less material, but no less life threatening. They are even more malevolent due to their subtlety.

Art history teaches that the truly lasting works of great art are those that wrestle with the confounding themes of existence. Humanity's relation to God, nature, war, sexuality, society, and self are the motifs repeated time and again. From the prehistoric cave paintings of France, to Michelangelo's Sistine Chapel, to Picasso's Guernica, to Dali's Last Supper, over and over the scenes are those of humankind's struggle to resolve conflict.

A mark of emotional and mental health is the ability to contend with the struggle and anguish of life. The person who comes to the art therapist, whether in private practice or in psychiatric hospital, regardless of diagnosis or personality type is one who is in conflict. They are those who have been unable to successfully cope, fully defend, or satisfactorily adapt. Their lives bear the scars of having been beaten and battered by their struggle with life.

The task of the art therapist is to call upon the inherent creative potential of the patient. We must enlist that creativity as an ally in the complicated task of unraveling the snarled yarn of the patient's life, freeing the person from the snare of victimization.

In my first year of graduate school I suffered from a malady common among my peers. I had the feeling that I was somehow less intelligent, less sophisticated than everyone else in school. For months I wrestled with whether or not I should drop out of school. I finally decided to share my concerns with my academic advisor. As I told him that I believed I was, "over my head," he began to laugh. I flushed with anger and resentment. Then he told me that I was the third student that week who was feeling overwhelmed.

"Bruce," he said. "You are suffering because you haven't figured out the higher education game yet. You see, it's not a matter of teaching students facts, or dates or even famous people's ideas. The point of being here is to learn how to learn." (Fig. 8).

A light came on in my head. I'd been focusing all of my attention on

Figure 8. Our primary task is doing creative work.

specifics of course material while ignoring the whole process of learning to think creatively about any given problem or situation.

As art therapists we are in an intriguing position with our patients. Our primary task is the doing of creative work with the arts. By so doing we call out the creative potential of our clients. As artists we know that conflict is inherent in painting, sculpting, molding, dancing and making. By virtue of all that has been created in the name of art we stand at a pivotal point in the acceptance and expression of conflict. Doing art is a natural method of evoking and sharing feelings and ideas which are essentially conflictual. As art therapists we foster in our patients a belief that they are capable of creative resolution of the problems of art production. At this same time the capability to struggle with other areas of conflict is serendipitously nourished.

Art therapists must not encourage the focusing of attention on one specific conflict, but rather on the nature of conflict as a symbol of life in process. If this attitude can be engendered in the patient then particular struggles will no longer be avoided, but embraced as a validation of life itself.

Chapter X

ART THERAPISTS AND SOCIAL RESPONSIBILITY

As an art therapist I believe that we have a serious responsibility to the world around us. It is not enough to learn your craft and practice it in isolation from culture. Because of our tradition of artistic struggle passed to us from all artists throughout history, coupled with our corporate concern for the well being of humanity we are compelled to be active agents for change.

Thirty years have passed since Dr. Erich Fromm wrote, *Man today is confronted with the most fundamental choice... between robotism (of both capitalist and communist variety) or Humanistic Communitarian Socialism. Most facts seem to indicate that he is choosing robotism and that means, in the long run, insanity and destruction. But all these facts are not strong enough to destroy faith in man's reason, good will and sanity. As long as we can think of alternatives, we are not lost. As long as we can consult together and plan together, we can hope. But indeed, the shadows are lengthening, the voices are becoming louder.* [15] Despite the events of intervening years I find myself listening keenly to Fromm's warning. The shadows have lengthened and the voices continue to rise.

I am reminded of some of the social sounds that I have heard these past four decades. Listen:

The war to end all wars came to a close.
The Korean War followed.
The Viet Nam War followed.
A voice cried in the wilderness
    I have a dream.
Other voices shouted,
America, Love it or Leave it.
Shots echoed in the streets of Dallas.
Shots echoed in the streets of Memphis.
Shots echoed in the streets of L. A.
Richard Nixon saw the light at the end of the tunnel.
The Beatles sang, *All you need is love.*
Mayor Daily demanded order in Chicago.

99

Governor Rhodes ordered National Guard troops
onto the Kent State University Campus.
Draft cards burned.
Gloria Steinem gave us a new image of women.
Carter announced there was a malaise upon the people.
It felt good if we did it.
Yuppies flourished.
We learned to drink Perrier.
Reagan decried, That Evil Empire.
The bulls thundered and the bears roared.
We were offered the image of a thousand points of light.
There would be no new taxes.
The Berlin Wall crumbled.
The Soviet Union tumbled.
The national debt skyrocketed
and on and on and on.

One attribute of our culture today is that we do not value pain. T. V. commercials assure us that pain is absolutely unnecessary. All one needs to do is take something. Pain is portrayed as something you get rid of. We like things to be easy. We like disposable things because they are so easy to live with, use them, throw them away. We like easy relationships, easy sex, easy fast food, easy abortion, easy divorce, easy entertainment, easy work. We like to take life easy and we all hope for an easy death.

If you enjoy dark comedy you can't help but like underarm deodorant commercials. One recent campaign slogan proclaimed, "never let 'em see you sweat." It takes no great psychoanalytical thinking to interpret the common message of both the pain reliever and deodorant commercials. "Don't put up with discomfort, and at all costs, don't let anyone know how you really feel."

In the hospital setting I have seen the terribly disturbed and lost find themselves again. I have seen those in excruciating pain cease their running, turn to face and tame their monsters. I have seen those who once lived only for the pleasures of the moment learn the deep joy of struggle. How? By doing art. The studio, whether it be a music practice room, a dance floor, a stage, or a room filled with empty canvases is a sanctuary. The studio protects the virtue of struggle and the value of pain. It is there that attempts are made, failures allowed, mastery accomplished through repetition of process, gratification delayed and occasional successes celebrated.

It is in the studio that the present day artist ties himself to the collective past of all artists before him. It is from the sum of all works of art, the tradition, that the artist makes his creative leap, taking his place in the long chain of art history.

The history of art is a saga of struggle, for the process of making art is like that of giving birth. An act of love, labor, and pain. From this tradition we art therapists must have an impact on life and society by taking every opportunity to remind people that it is OK to hurt. It is good to struggle, and that life is hard.

Chapter XI

PROCESS AND PRODUCT

In one of the very early documents describing the psychotherapeutic use of art, Don Jones, A. T. R., H. L. M., wrote, *Emphasis must be placed on the process not the product. A simple stick figure may be more meaningful than an elaborate painting.* [16]

This view of the components of therapeutic art work has, for the most part, gone unchallenged over the past twenty-five years as the profession has developed in the United States. Evidence of the continued dominance of this position is seen annually at the national conferences of the American Art Therapy Association. Reproductions of patient art products are often presented in slides of poor quality, and the art pieces themselves tend toward rough and aesthetically impoverished works. At the same time, art therapists' discussions of the art have focused on them as being exemplary illustrations of pathology, personality deviance and analytical intrigue.

Further indications of the bias regarding the value of process over product can be gathered by review of the abstracts prepared for the A. A. T. A. conference proceedings. Seldom have the topics of the aesthetics of the patient-artist, or the art therapist as artist been addressed. This is not to say that there have not been notable exceptions to this, but by and large the professional gatherings of art therapists have been devoid of reference to the quality of art, whether by patient or therapist. Interestingly, it was Don Jones who, (to the best of my knowledge), first introduced slides of his own paintings in a presentation titled, *A Professional Looks Back,* [17] several years ago.

More recently art therapists have stepped to the forefront of this issue by publicly displaying their products as artists in presentations, publications and by exhibiting their work. In *Existential Art Therapy: The Canvas Mirror,* I stated, "It is essential to remain active artistically if we are to stay honest in our profession. The dangers of not doing so are many, but most significant is the damage that artistic inactivity does to the authenticity of the art therapist." [3] This was followed by a subsection *Images From the Mirror,* in which I presented 17 paintings as a plea for artist-therapists to return to their studios.

In his most recent book, *Art as Medicine,*[18] Shaun McNiff devotes the last 81 pages of the text to *Image Dialogues,* exploring the messages of his paintings. A meta-message of this segment of the book is that he is confident of his proficiency as an artist and is willing to withstand the potential criticism that the inclusion of his products may allow.

In 1989 art therapists, Debra DeBrular and Cathy Moon staged a two woman show of paintings, sculpture and quilts, in the exhibit hall of the Methodist Theological School in Ohio. In this instance their focus was not on art work done by art therapists, but rather works created by two women artists.

In an article in the Journal of the American Art Therapy Association, Ms. Pat Allen (Ph.D.) offered a model for art therapists which she termed, "The Artist in Residence." The essence of her proposal is that art therapists reclaim their tradition of artist and avoid the complications of becoming overly *clinified.*[19]

Each of the above examples, and there are no doubt many more throughout the country, point to a growing movement in the art therapy profession which is reclaiming the role of the artist as a crucial aspect of our professional personality.

It is puzzling that such a movement should be necessary at all in a profession in which the first word of its name is ART. It is my sense that the art appellation lost its significance as the profession moved to define itself in the company of psychiatry, psychology and social work. Perhaps unintentionally, as early leaders of the discipline struggled for professional recognition and prestige, efforts were made to master the language of these other, more well established, occupations. It was as if art therapists longed to be regarded as equivalent to the physician, psychologist and family therapist. While it is easy to understand the motivations of those in the forefront of such efforts as the field of art therapy developed, it is also easy to see, in retrospect, that much of our unique identity as artist-therapists was abandoned along the way. The motives for being like psychiatry or psychology are apparent: Increased earning potential, potential administrative influence, employability, and professional prestige. Each of these are powerful persuaders that lured the art therapy profession away from its roots in the art world. What has emerged is a generation of art therapists fluent in statistical study, psychological jargon, and political savvy, but insecure regarding the integral place of the arts in the treatment of human suffering.

Despite the encouraging signs noted above regarding the resurgence of the role of aesthetics in the professional life of the art therapist there remains much division regarding this issue. Many in the profession continue to insist that art therapy must imitate other health care disciplines. This is evidenced in the guidelines for approval of Master's level academic programs and Clinical Training Programs published by the American Art Therapy Association and overseen by the Education and Training Board of the A. A. T. A.

The power and depth of artistic expression demands that we art therapists be sensitive to nuances of color and shade, the push and pull of emotional currents that course through line character, and the aesthetic sensibilities inherent in the balancing of weight and mass. Those who would become art therapists should resist the temptations to aspire to the lifestyle of the physician, or the institutional political power of the psychologist. Students of the field should instead insist that they be trained as art therapists and nothing less than that.

The art therapy profession must be connected to the sensual. The core of our work revolves around sight, sound, movement and touch. This establishes an inherent tension between art therapists and members of other verbally oriented disciplines for our primary therapeutic language cannot be found in a dictionary. Our language is found in studios, exhibitions and museums. It is time for art therapists to abandon pursuits that lead us to become pseudo-psychiatrists. We must turn back to our heritage in the arts.

The Anguish of Aaron

Aaron came to my private practice office with the complaint that he was, "always depressed and worried." A pleasant and gentle man in his mid '30s, Aaron had been treated for alcoholism at a residential center for several weeks the year prior. In our intake session he told me he had remained sober for thirteen months and that although he felt positively about not drinking, he simply could not shake the feelings of emptiness and pointlessness that plagued him.

Aaron told me that he was in his second year of graduate school and that he was going to complete his Masters in Business Administration in the spring. He was unmarried and, "on the rebound," from an intense relationship with a woman whom he had planned to marry. She had left him for another man.

I asked Aaron what he hoped to get out of coming to see me.

"I am not sure. A friend suggested that I try art therapy and I got your name from the hospital. I feel like I've tried a lot of other stuff, why not this?"

I asked again, "What do you hope for from our relationship?"

He sat silent for a moment. "I guess I want to get control of myself. I want to feel better."

I handed him a large pad of newsprint and a box of pastel chalks. "Aaron, I'm not sure that I am willing to see you for therapy. It would help me if you would draw a portrait of how you feel."

He shook his head in surprise. "What do you mean you aren't sure you'll see me in therapy? Why?"

"Well, this practice is very small and I can only work with a very few patients at a time. I have to be sure that you really want to do the work that you say you want to do. Now would you please start your drawing?"

Although he looked as if he had many more questions he began to work. Aaron drew a circle, about two inches in diameter in the lower right hand side of the page. Then using black chalk he covered the rest of the sheet of newsprint. In the middle of the untouched circle he scribbled an intense red asterisk. In less than five minutes he handed the pad back to me, saying that he was finished. The design was visually interesting but his handling of the media was slipshod. As a result of his careless application of the chalk the image seemed messy, and incoherent.

Without commenting on the drawing I asked Aaron how his grades were and if he liked graduate school. Although he clearly liked the idea of having a masters degree, his answers hinted that he was doing just enough to get by and that he did not particularly enjoy his studies. He then initiated a long story of how he had begun to drink in his early 'teens. He essentially recited the work that he had done in completing the first step of Alcoholics Anonymous.

I asked, "Were you good at drinking?"

He looked at me incredulously. "What kind of a question is that?"

"Were you good at drinking?" I asked again.

Aaron's face reddened. "Well, I guess so. But what's that have to do with anything?" His voice had an irritated edge.

I placed his drawing on the floor between our two chairs. "You seem to want to hurry through things, Aaron. Like your drawing here. I didn't put any time limits on how long you could work. The task was to draw a portrait of how you've been feeling. By your own account you've been feeling sad and empty for a long time; it was surprising to me that you could draw such profound feelings so quickly."

"I don't get this!" He exclaimed.

I said, "Aaron, I wanted to know if you were good at drinking because I am interested in things that you really have paid attention to, and taken your time on, in your life."

"I don't see what in the hell this has to do with anything?"

I looked at him thoughtfully for a moment. "Aaron, I am willing to see you in therapy on one condition, that you commit yourself to working diligently with art."

"Why?" He wanted to know.

"I think that you already know a lot about your feelings but you don't seem to think much of yourself. What I have to offer you, as an art therapist, is my willingness to help you work with the images that are inside you. I believe that they have things to teach you, but you have to handle them with care and respect. That means taking your time, attending to them."

Aaron looked down at his chalk drawing. "I don't want to sound rude Mr. Moon, but it almost seems like you care more about my picture than me. I think maybe I've made a mistake. I don't think you'll be able to help me."

"You are probably right, Aaron. If you don't believe that I can be of help then I certainly won't be. It's your choice. Why don't you think about it for awhile, give me a call if you want to start. If I don't hear from you in a couple of weeks I'll assume that you have decided against working with me."

As Aaron left the office that afternoon he took his drawing with him, but I was relatively sure that I would not hear from him again. Nearly six months had passed when he called to set up another appointment.

He asked, "When would be a good time for me to come to your office?"

"Do you really want to work with me in art therapy?"

"Yes, that's why I called you."

"Then meet me at the studio (I gave him directions) at 7:00 Thursday night."

He immediately began to ask why we would not be getting together at the office, what we would be doing, how he should dress, etc. etc. I told him that I wanted to teach him to paint, and that he should come wearing clothes that he wouldn't mind getting dirty.

Aaron arrived at the studio promptly. He looked around for a minute or two, taking in the paintings that hang on the walls, the sculptures that clutter the benches, all the artifacts of patients past and present that adorn the space.

Enthusiastically he said, "What am I going to paint first?"

"I don't know," I replied. "All that we are going to do tonight is build the canvas."

With slightly less eagerness he said, "So, where do we start?"

I pulled two 2 × 2s from the wood rack and said, "Since this is your first painting let's start small. I'd like you to measure two pieces twenty-four inches long, and two pieces twenty-eight inches long." I handed him a tape measure and carpenters pencil.

When he had finished marking the wood he asked, "Now what?"

I gestured toward the hand miter box and said, "Set the angle for 45° and cut each end of your 2 × 2s."

(I was operating on a hunch that Aaron had not had many experiences in his life with hand tools or building processes. Likewise I suspected that he had not experienced parallel play/work situations with his father. It was my belief that he was hungry for positive encounters with an accepting male who would do things with him.)

I watched as he approached the miter box tentatively. It was clear that he did not know where to position the 2 × 2, nor how to place his hands so that he could both operate the saw and clamp the piece of wood to the metal back wall of the miter box. He also seemed unsure of how to adjust the angle mechanism of the saw.

Without commenting on his lack of knowledge regarding the saw and box, I showed Aaron how to change the angle and how to position the wood. I left the sawing to him. He began to pull the saw hesitantly. "It won't bite." I said.

Without stopping he replied, "I've never done this before."

"You are doing just fine, Aaron. Just fine."

When all his cuts were made I gave him a piece of coarse sandpaper and suggested that he smooth the edges that he'd just cut.

"Why, they aren't going to show, are they?"

"No, they won't show, but they will fit together more snugly. You'll feel better about the joints if they are clean and tight. There is no substitute for quality."

"This is taking longer than I thought." He sighed. "I thought I'd be painting something tonight."

As I continued to work on the stretcher frame that I was building I said, "Aaron, you have got to learn the five Ps. Patience and planning provides for positive performance. Building stretchers is all about patience."

"But couldn't I just go to the store and buy a canvas that is already stretched and painted white?"

"Sure you could," I said, "but you can't do that and work with me."

He wanted to know why.

"Because if you buy a pre-stretched, pre-gessoed canvas you've already cut yourself off from the process. You miss an opportunity to be in touch with the soul of the painting."

When each of the angled cuts had been sanded I showed Aaron how to clamp two pieces together in order to nail them securely. After he put the last nail in he held the rectangular frame up for inspection. It was clearly a moment of gratification and pride for him.

"Does the canvas go on now?"

"No," I said. "First we need to use the carpenters square to check all of the corners, then we'll make a couple angle braces to make sure that the frame doesn't distort when we stretch the canvas."

By the time this procedure was completed Aaron's hour was nearly finished. "Aaron, we should discuss the financial arrangements for your therapy. There are a couple options.

"Oh yeah, I almost forgot about that part."

"If you would like to use your medical insurance the fee will be $60 per session. I'll expect you to pay $30 at the end of each session. The rest you will pay me when you get reimbursed by the insurance company."

He thought for a moment. "I think I'd like to avoid the insurance company. If I use them I'll have to talk with my employer again. That got a little embarrassing last year. How does payment work if I don't use insurance?"

"I work on a sliding scale, so it depends upon how much you earn. For instance, if you make thirty thousand dollars a year my charge will be $30 per session. If you make fifty thousand, it will be $50. The most I charge anybody is $70, and the least I work for is $25. So, you tell me how much you owe me."

Aaron wrote a check for forty-five dollars. He said, "You talk about the bill very nicely. One of my other counselors always hemmed and hawed about money. He seemed embarrassed."

"I don't mind talking about the fee at all. I believe in the product you are purchasing. I know that I will give you the best quality service at my disposal."

In a variety of ways this session set the tone for the rest of the time I spent in Aaron's life. Our interactions focused most often on the tasks at hand, stretching canvas, planning the painting, technical details, and finally framing and setting hanging wire on the back. Each step in the process, from gathering tools and materials, through signing and displaying the finished product, was done with care and concern for quality. It must be noted here that Aaron did not come to me with a sense of himself as an adequate artist. In fact the opposite is nearer the truth. He came bearing his emptiness and self-loathing. In this case it was critical to engage him at the level he desperately longed for. It was necessary to help him develop a more positive regard for himself through doing. Mastery of task, coupled with self expression, was the treatment of choice for Aaron.

The poet, philosopher, therapist to the masculine spirit, Robert Bly has pointed out that prior to the industrial revolution little boys got to spend time in the company of their fathers as the father plowed the field, or worked in the shop, or built the house. This provided boys with experiences that taught them what it meant to be a man, experiences that initiated them into manhood. However, in the modern era, few such opportunities exist between fathers and sons. This leaves the son with an empty hunger for masculine relationships[20] (Fig. 9).

The therapy for Aaron, stemming from a Bly understanding of his core issues, became the doing together, taking care to invest attention to the quality of the work. By doing so Aaron got to experience the healing effects of being in the company of an older male who did not judge nor abandon him, plus the therapeutic effect of the expressive arts processes. In addition he developed a genuinely more positive internal view of himself as he worked with and gained mastery over materials and procedures.

The third painting that he worked on during his art therapy journey illustrates this with poignancy.

It was a large work, approximately 3′ × 4′. The scene was of a stark white house, bathed in bluish green light from a street lamp. The night sky was very dark, and a woman stood in the open doorway, dressed in a

Figure 9. This leaves the son with an empty hunger.

red, half-open robe. She appeared to be searching the darkness, looking for something or someone. The painting seemed cold, yet it had a quality of passion and expectancy.

The first time that I saw it in progress the sky was painted a dull black. It appeared flat and empty. "Aaron, do you want the sky to look dead?"

He shook his head. "No, but I want it to be really dark. I tried to mix up a midnight blue, but I couldn't get it the way I wanted, so I gave up."

I studied the painting intently. "Well, I think we ought to back up and make a dark blue for the sky. It really needs more depth than the flat black can give it."

"But I've already painted the sky. Do you know how much paint it took to cover all that canvas?" He raised his voice. "Do you know how long it took to paint it black?"

"It doesn't matter how long, or how much paint it took, Aaron. It doesn't look right. There is no substitute for quality work. Now what colors did you use to try to mix midnight blue?"

He told me that he had blended cobalt blue with warm black.

"Oh," I said. "That was the problem. Let's try it again, only this time use ultramarine blue as the base.

"I really think that this is a waste of time and money. I already used a lot of black."

"I'll be glad to help you Aaron. But I won't do it for you. You know this reminds me of other things you've said about your life. Now, c'mon and start mixing paint."

As he squeezed ultramarine blue onto the palette he asked, "So what is that supposed to mean? It reminds you of other parts of my life."

"Yes. You've told me several stories from your relationship with Annie (his former girlfriend), from work, and from grad school where the whole point was how much you regret that you did not do things more carefully, take your time and do it right."

Aaron was clearly irritated with how the session was proceeding. "Yea, give me one example." His voice held a defensive edge.

I thought for a moment. "Well, how about the Managerial Time Study Project, that you told me about a couple of weeks ago. You told me yourself that you hurried. The result was a B, and you said that you knew you could have gotten an A if you had really applied yourself."

He dropped the paint stir in an exasperated motion. "So what. That was no big deal. My life doesn't revolve around a Managerial Time Study on a fictitious corporation."

"No, Aaron. You are right. But the point is that if you handle the little things in a sloppy manner, it is likely that you'll treat more important things in the same way."

"Ah bull!"

"Another example, and maybe a more important one, is how you described your intimacies with Annie."

"What in the world are you talking about?"

"Well, you told me that when you look back you think that you were only interested in your own pleasure, not hers. You said, 'I just hurried through all the preliminaries,' and eventually that backfired."

In a hostile and sarcastic voice he replied, "So you think that taking time to mix paint will bring Annie back?"

I spoke softly. "No, but it might help you to pay more attention the next time around." There was a long pause. "I think you've gotten into the habit of rushing through life, Aaron, without focusing on anything. You are a sort of mediocre Jack-of-all-trades. Is the dark blue ready? I think that your life deserves more care than you have given it. There is no substitute for quality work."

The sky was repainted. When he completed covering the black with the dark blue he decided to paint in an orange-white harvest moon. Having done that he added touches of moonlight on the grass outside the house, small highlights on the woman's face and on her robe. Aaron allowed himself to work for a few months on the painting. He made some mistakes, got frustrated, but was able to back up, think things through and then rework the images until he was satisfied. In a parallel sense this describes what Aaron was doing intrapsychically, i.e., learning to struggle with attending to himself. He made some errors, became irritated, but was able to stop and gather himself, and remake his self image. He learned to like what he saw in the canvas mirror.

I do not believe that such work could have been done in verbal psychotherapy. It was essential that Aaron encounter himself through the experience of making art. This is not to diminish the therapeutic benefit of the relationship that we developed over time. Certainly this had its curative impact as well, but even our relationship was intimately connected to the creative process and mastery of materials. It was in the context of the studio that our relationship existed.

It was equally significant that I insisted that he struggle with style and technique. Throughout our relationship I demanded that he use materials in a manner that honored them. Had I been willing to accept whatever artistic endeavor Aaron offered I believe I would have exacerbated his negative self view for he would have known that I was willing to settle for less than his best attempt. There would have been no motivation on his part to struggle. That was the heart of his discomfort.

As art therapists we have the unique capacity to relate simultaneously with *the patient, the process, the image and the product.* This capacity allows us to move between the positions of consoler, teacher, beholder, and critic.

In the lives of many patients and clients the longing for meaning is a critical element of their *dis-ease.* As an art therapist I believe that the role of art is a profound factor in establishing a sense of purposefulness. When the artist has genuinely struggled with the creative process and allowed the flow of imagery to proceed from within, he has said, in his most honest and clear voice, "This is who and what I am."

Nietzsche said, "Only artists dare to show us the human being as he is." For too long, in the art therapy profession, there has been a tendency to avoid looking too closely at the unique and authentic gifts of our, and our patient's art works from an aesthetic perspective. It is critical that this oversight be corrected in order for art therapy to thrive. It is the aesthetics of the profession which depend most intimately on the image and the product, the lasting artifacts of the work. Processes, images, and their inevitable products distinguish the practice of art therapy from the routines of psychiatry, psychology and social work.

Chapter XII

CURATIVE ASPECTS OF ART IN THERAPY

How does art therapy help clients and patients? This is in some ways a naive question, yet if it can be answered with any sense of certainty, the art therapy profession will clearly have a critical coordinate from which to map its approach to the disturbing and unclear dilemmas of psychotherapy. If they can be observed and described, the essential elements of the role art plays in the process of facilitating therapeutic change will form a logical foundation from which art therapists may construct treatment plans and philosophies.

The course of change in therapy is an intricate and nearly indefinable process. Change happens in the context of a complex weaving of relationship and experience. In the art therapy milieu the relationships are multiple: patient to therapist, patient to materials, patient to tools, patient to images and therapist to patient—materials—tools—and images. Experiences are also multiple—tactile, visual, and process oriented. The intersections between relationships and experiences are the locations where the curative aspects of art therapy are formed.

If a carpenter attempts to describe the process of building a house in its entirety the discourse must inevitably be overwhelmingly complex and technical. However, if the same carpenter explains the use of 2 × 4s in the construction of walls, the description will be relatively easy to digest and understand. Whenever attempting to describe the complicated it is helpful to explore first the simplest building blocks. An intricate whole may best be understood through its basic parts. Following this logic I will turn to discussing the curative aspects of art in therapy.

From my perspective the healing elements may be partitioned in the following fashion.

1. Art as Existentialism
2. Art as Communication
3. Art as Soul

4. Art as Mastery
5. Art as Personal Metaphor
6. Art as Empowerment
7. Art as Work
8. Art as Play
9. Art as Relationship
10. Art as Structure and Chaos
11. Art as Hope
12. Art as Benevolence

1. **Art as Existentialism.** The art psychotherapy process is a difficult one. Most often it is begun as the patient or client is in the midst of painful and frightening life crises. The particular events and circumstances that lead a person to seek art therapy are as diverse as the individuals themselves. However, there are common threads that appear time and again. Existential therapists and philosophers describe these as the *ultimate concerns of existence.* Prominent among them are; freedom, aloneness, guilt, each person's responsibility for her own life, the inevitability of suffering and death, and a deep longing for meaning.

Existential art therapists focus their work in addressing the patient's anxieties and defense mechanisms which form in response to an awareness of the ultimate concerns of life. They view their work as tied to the creative struggle with the core issues of meaning, isolation, freedom, and death (Fig. 10).

The essence of existential art therapy is found in the visual image. In practice the art therapist working from this perspective attends to the patient by (1) doing with them, (2) being open to them, and (3) honoring their pain.

Artists have always known that a primary source of their creative work is their own emotional turmoil stimulated by their struggle with the ultimate concerns. A key notion in existential therapy is that people relate to these issues either by attempting to ignore them, or by living in what Irvin Yalom refers to as, *a state of mindfulness.*[21] It is the awareness of our capacity to be self-creative in the state of mindfulness which promotes the ability to change. The arts are natural activities for expression. Expression leads to mindfulness.

The major thrust of my work as an existential art therapist can be conceptualized as going on a shared journey with the patient. The purpose of this pilgrimage is to discover the meanings of the patient's

Figure 10. . . . the core issues of meaning, isolation and death.

life as emerging in artistic processes and products. I guard against the temptations to become an interpreter or diagnostician. Rather I encourage the patient to make his own interpretations, to become his own analyst and analysand.

Throughout history the arts have always dealt with the ultimate concerns of existence. It is this tradition of struggle that is the extraordinary gift of the artist therapist. Artists have always struggled with issues of meaning, isolation, death and creative freedom. As art therapists it is our mandate to do the same in the company of our fellow travelers. Making art is a process of dealing with existential concerns.

2. **Art as Communication.** Every time the painter fills her brush and moves it across the canvas, every time the author pounds the keys of his typewriter, every time the poet scrawls her rhyme, every time the trumpeter wets his lips, these artists proclaim to the world, *I am here ... I have something to say, I am.* As the audience beholds these proclamations they bring honor to the tired muscles, the hours of practice, and the deep feelings that have conspired together to create.

In the therapeutic arts studio, drawings, sculptures and paintings provide the patient and therapist with snapshots of inner life. Each line, each shape, and each color are pieces of realities that defy verbal description.

The etiology of words suggests that all language was once expressive and imaginative. It is clear, however, that both the spoken and written words have lost much of their original power to evoke. Parallel to the phenomenon of the weakening of words has been a diminishment in the general populace of meaningful use of imaginative and creative capacities. Add to this a cultural trend toward avoidance of feelings, reflection and sharing, and one is left with a patient population that has had little contact with authentic expression. Validation of this can be found in the popular beer commercial slogan, *Why ask why?* The implicit message being, don't think too deeply about your life, drink instead.

For many patients, whether in psychiatric hospitals, out patient clinics, pastoral care centers or wellness programs, the therapeutic arts may offer an authentic communication mode sorely lacking in their lives.

As the patient paints in my presence I am keenly aware of her relationship to the processes, materials and images that emerge. With each brush stroke the patient is telling her tale, setting the stage for the sharing of stories that is the basis of the art psychotherapy pilgrimage. These communications are often raw and painful, but always encouraging to me. As art therapists we must be open to understanding what has been expressed. By doing so, a safe milieu in which patient artists may engage in self-exploration is established. Art is communication.

3. **Art as Soul.** The first time that I can remember ever hearing *art* and *soul* mentioned in the same sentence was in a conversation with a patient sometime in the late '70s. She said, "My pictures are the windows to my soul." I do not think that I understood her at that time. I thought she was merely being poetic. As is often the case, it has taken me a long time to understand the truth of her words (Fig. 11).

Figure 11. ... pictures are the windows to my soul.

The notion of art and soul being in some intimate relationship slept undisturbed within me for years after this fleeting conversation. It was reawakened in the mid '80s by the works of Shaun McNiff and Cathy Moon. In his *Depth Psychology of Art* [22] Shaun worked with the nomenclature of our profession and asserted that we must, "reclaim our roots in a view of the arts as an unconscious religion."[22] He also brought to the fore the interrelationship of psyche and soul and posited that images are the expressions of soul.

Cathy presented a paper to the American Art Therapy Association national conference at about that same time entitled, *Art as Prayer.*[23] This was, I believe, the first presentation at the national level which had as its focus an exploration of the common ground between the arts, therapy and spirituality. Since then there has been an ever increasing level of interest in such matters.

When the therapeutic arts in the hospital or clinic setting are regarded from a perspective of *soul,* the work is made sacred. From this perspective patients' images cannot be seen as pathological, but rather as heartfelt portraits of selfhood. I embrace the belief that art comes from the depths of human experience, out of passion, conflict and creative turmoil.

Making art is making soul. Art processes offer a new perspective, an imaginative portrait of the artist. Painting, drawing, and sculpture make meanings visible by turning random events into ensouled experiences. There is an artistic substructure to human existence that cannot be pinpointed as the property of behavior or language or physiology. The exceptional gift of art therapists to the patient and to the clinical setting is the soul/art making process. This is work that only art therapists can do.

Images and metaphors present themselves as living psychic subjects with which I am obliged to be in relation. . . . A particular image is a necessary angel waiting for a response.[10]

Regardless of the form one's faith finds, Judaic, Christian, Zen, Islamic, or secular humanism it is reflected in the art we create. As an art therapist I view the work I do as a sacred journey that my patients and I go on together. Our mode of transportation is the doing of artistic work. Our primary mode of communication is the sharing of images that we create in the context of our relationship. These are the visual parables and prayers, *angels* that mark the pilgrimage. In the sanctuary of our studios souls are made in the midst of imaged confessions, thanksgivings, and praises. It is a sacred thing to be an art therapist, for the doing of art opens to us the mystery that is within our patients and ourselves. It is a sacred thing to look through the soul windows of others. Making art is making soul (Fig. 12).

4. **Art as Mastery.** It is essential that art therapists possess a profound respect for the work, *mastery,* of art processes and materials. This rever-

Figure 12. Making art is making soul.

ence must be applied to the image, the patient, and the efforts of the therapist. It will be evidenced in the drive toward mastery of both patient/artist and artist/therapist. The sense of adequacy that comes from mastery of artistic techniques and media is linked to self-discipline and inevitably leads to positive self-regard. From this comes a sacred passion for life. This sacred passion is disclosed through authentic, creative and vital interactions between the individual and the world. Such interactions are inherently connected to the artist's skillful use of media. Of course, technical competence is hollow without the emotional investment of the artist. Still, the success of any art work depends equally upon its communication of feeling and its demonstration of capable handling of materials.

As art therapists we must not rely exclusively upon the passing cathartic expressions of our patients. We must also address the authority of formal artistic procedures on the quality of expression. Careful attention must be given to the constant evolution of our mastery of art processes. These are as important as our interpersonal relationship skills, communications skills, understanding of personality and psychotherapeutic techniques.

In a deep sense, mastery may be described as the ability to organize and transform both raw materials, and experiences. The significance of art work in the psychotherapeutic setting is found as patients transform powerful destructive inner forces into constructive, meaningful objects. The process of making art is a process of organizing chaotic emotional material into a coherent, restructured product. The turbulent swirl of feelings, sensations, actions and relationships are the markers of mental and emotional distress. The arts offer hope for clarity and balance by alleviating the distress through the work itself.

As the patient's awareness of mastery grows in relation to a specific artistic task there is always a corresponding increase in confidence and self-esteem. A reciprocity is thus established between the artist, the task, and the product that is intra-psychically contagious. As the patient artist experiences success in his ability to handle media and solve artistic problems, the capacity to deal with other aspects of his life is enhanced.

I am proposing here that we art therapists take the quality of our patients art work, and our own, seriously. At every opportunity we must encourage our patients not only to vent their feelings, but to do so in a skillful and artistically articulate manner.

I have worked with many patients who initially used the arts studio as a sort of dumping ground for feelings they wished not to have. These persons often completed one or more paintings in an hour and a half session. These products frequently resembled mud. In such instances my response has been to insist that they stop regurgitating and learn the mechanics of mixing color. Other patients have benefited from lessons in one and two point perspective. These disciplines have helped the patient structure and organize their expression in a way that allows personal attachment to both the process and the final product. This is not to say that I insist on pleasant or pretty pictures. On the contrary, most times the images that are born in the studio are painful and raw, but I do insist on attention to quality in the work itself.

My contention that attention to quality must be given is based on the belief that mastery equals care. If I allow my patient to simply slop paint onto a canvas, with no regard to the quality of the work then I would essentially be telling them that I have no investment in their art, and *ergo* no real interest in them. Likewise, if I approach my own artistic efforts in the therapeutic studio with anything less than a focused care in relation to quality, I would be modeling inattention to self.

I do not necessarily expect my patients to become accomplished artists, but I do expect them to learn to care about quality in their lives. I ask them to do the best work that they can, and I look for ways to help them be better than they believe they are capable of being. Making art is working toward mastery.

5. **Art as Personal Metaphor.** A metaphor is a manner of speaking in which one thing is described in the terms of another. The bringing together of the two sheds new light on the character of that which is being described and holds in tension the possibility of multiple interpretations.

While the above description adequately addresses the verbal dimensions of metaphor, it is an insufficient definition for creative arts therapists. For our work, the idea of metaphor as image and action is much more satisfactory. In this sense metaphors are images that hold symbolic meanings, both conscious and unconscious, for the artist. Their purpose is to articulate, express, free and define their creator. This is an essential element of our discipline.

Metaphoric images contain an inherent quality of comparison in which one thing (the art object) is used to shed new light on the character of the artist. The reverse is, of course, also true. Just as verbal metaphors hold the possibility of many divergent interpretations, so it is with visual and action metaphors.

As art therapists we are in an extraordinary position to see and respond to the metaphoric creations of our patients. We must honor the view of the poet, Rilke, who posited that art interprets itself. This suggests that the proper response to a painting is not analyzing its line quality, or its form relationships, but rather by painting another painting, or writing a song, or making an enactment. We must not attempt to enslave it through our vocabulary. Rather we should promote an appreciation, an awe and dedicate ourselves to the notion that images can, and should just *be*.

Everything we create are partial attempts at self portraiture. By this I do not mean to imply that this is all that images are, but it is one important aspect that is of deep therapeutic and clinical interest to art therapists. We need only to look at, and be with, our patient's images. We hardly need to talk at all.

The need to put images and experiences into words is an aspect of the art therapy profession that repeatedly makes me uncomfortable with my colleagues. It seems to imply that the art therapist does not trust the image to convey its own meanings. It is fundamental that art therapists value the communication that is presented in the artistic process and product. This is so despite the fact that images hold the potential for multiple interpretations, thus leaving us with only ambiguous, mysterious and unconfirmed responses. Making art is making personal metaphor.

6. **Art as Empowerment.** In most instances the persons who come to the art therapist as outpatients, or who are hospitalized in a treatment facility, whether for psychiatric or physical reasons, come with a sense of disenfranchisement. Their belief in their personal power has been wounded. They often feel victimized by family, friends or the world itself. It is an essential task of the art therapist to work with the patient to restore their awareness and faith in their own power.

Empowerment is not a process that can be accomplished through verbalization alone. There must be experiences that foster the reclamation of power and the responsibilities that accompany it.

Art therapists are in an ideal position to facilitate the process of empowerment in our patients by virtue of our own experiences with imagery. It is true that we are first initiated into the healing and transformative nature of artistic work through our own empowering engagements with media and processes. Art brings meaning to life by transforming conflict and ennobling painful struggle. Struggle is an essential element of human nature. The collision of internal forces is what brings about the creative actions of art. Our primary task is to inspire in the patient the desire to *use* his discomfort, rather than be abused by it. The act of empowerment is a process of transformation from the position of the victim, to the position of the hero/survivor.

Human beings are a conglomerate of opposing forces, inconsistencies and contradictions. We are in a state of continual change. Conflict and struggle are inevitable. There is a core tension within the self that is most clearly expressed through our polarities. Art does not lessen the tension; on the contrary, it often accentuates it by using the energy in empowering actions. Artists bring meaning in their lives as they shape and color the distressing disharmony within them. Creation does not banish pain or discomfort but rather ensouls it. Through the creative process of art-making, contradictions and conflicts are brought into clear focus that makes non-logical sense. The empowering nature of art therapy does not seek cures, it accepts and ennobles. Art brings our deepest fears, loneliness and anguish close to us. It does not rid us of these difficulties; rather it enables us to live courageously in their presence.

The very process of creating art is a metaphor for life itself in that as the artist works she has ultimate power to change the picture. She can add new color, darken or highlight. The artist can, if she chooses, paint over the piece and start again. This is an allegory of life itself. It can be changed, if and when the individual decides to change. Many times the patient does not believe that she has such power over the course of her own life. So the doing of art becomes an introduction into free will and the power of choice and creation. Making art empowers.

7. **Art as Work.** The sum of an artist's production is described as his, or her, work. The body of this work is the aggregate of the artist's capacity to put forth effort, toil and exhibit patience as the labor unfolds. It is a concrete measure of the artist's tolerance of the internal dynamism that both seethes and soothes. It is unfortunate that the public so often sees only the finished work, and not the work that was required prior to display. The labor of artists is not easy nor comfortable. There are many sore muscles, strained eyes, blistered hands and hearts that must conspire to create.

In art therapy it is essential that there be a profound respect for the art of both patient and therapist. The art therapist must not depend exclusively upon the impermanent cathartic efforts of the patient. Consideration must also be given to the weight of rigorous artistic technique on the quality of the expression. Such labors demand passionate discipline on the part of the art therapist. The patient's willingness to take the therapeutic journey is directly influenced by the enthusiasm and order of the therapist. The art therapist's passionate discipline can be seen nowhere clearer than in his, or her, own art work.

As we paint, or draw, or sculpt, we rediscover the meaning of our work as art therapists. It is in our own studio that we experience the struggle and confusion, the artistic frustrations that are integral to our work. Art is work.

8. **Art as Play.** Much of the time the work of art therapists involves being with patients' images that are raw, painful and horrific. These images come from the depths of persons who are struggling with their lives. It must be noted also, however, that the doing of art is fun. For all of our shadows and demons there are surely heroes and jesters lurking within, awaiting their turn on the imaginal stage. As art therapists we must have faith that they are as willing to share their joys as freely as the monsters dispense their terrors. This is why the faces of children light up as their crayon scribble is taped to the refrigerator door. This is the fun.

The grown up patient artists that I treat in my work at Harding Hospital, and in my private practice, are pointedly aware of the pain and discomfort that emerges in their images but it is fun, the play of the activity itself that enables the artist to face time and again the disturbing load of their creating.

Playing artistically offers a dynamic source of energy. There is a whimsical quality to art that allows emotion and mystery into the realm of daily life. This infusion of the magical and imaginal brightens the routine and familiar. An inherent aspect of art is that it brings pleasure, allowing us to contend with, and take part in, life. Playing encourages freedom and limits, thus promoting both work and action. Making art is playing (Figs. 13 & 14).

9. **Art as Relationship.** No matter where one looks in the history of humanity it is clear that relationships between individuals is of critical importance. This is evident whether we examine the development of one single person, or the evolution of a group, nation or entire culture.

In commenting on the dilemma between human beings serving their own interests and conforming to the interests of the group to which they belong, W. Goldschmidt stated, *... each person craves response from his human environment... Under varying conditions it may be expressed as a*

Figure 13. Making art is playing.

Figure 14. Making art is playing.

desire for contact, for recognition and acceptance, for approval, for esteem, or for mastery. [24]

This can be validated from the perspective of the art historian. Why else would prehistoric humans stain the walls of caves? Why else would Rouault paint, or Rodin sculpt? The act of making is an invitation to relate. By making, the artist takes images from within, and spreads them in the world. It is an act of acknowledgment of the *other* beyond the boundaries of the self. The *other* is the beholder, the audience.

There are few things more painful to the psyche than loneliness. This is evidenced by the fact that nearly every primary cause of death has been shown to be meaningfully higher for those who live alone.

Every major trend in psychotherapy, with the exception of psychopharmacology, is anchored in interpersonal theory. It may be argued that *all* therapy is relationship based, both in objective and approach.

Irvin D. Yalom states, *The theory of interpersonal relationships is presently so much an integral part of the fabric of psychiatric thought that it needs no underscoring. People need people—for initial and continued survival, for socialization, for the pursuit of satisfaction. No one—neither the dying, nor the outcast, nor the mighty—transcends the need for human contact.*[21]

Personal meaning can be found only in the context of relationship. The self must be transcended for purpose to be present. The creative process is best acknowledged in the domain of relatedness. Art is inspired in the territory of interpersonal connection which is the shared human experience. Whether in praise or critique it is the community that must respond to the artist and his work in order for the art process to be complete.

Through the work the artist offers his view, his unique response to the world. Although passive, the community receives the imaginal offspring of the artist's struggle. It is only in the context of relationship to the community that the artist establishes his particular self. The *other* comprehends the uniqueness of the artist. The artist creates, the community responds, the artist makes again and the community attends, and on and on the creative relating circle spins. Art making is relating.

10. **Art as Structure and Chaos.** My patients often tell me that the most difficult stage of their artistic journey is the beginning. As they stare at the white, empty canvas they are overwhelmed by the possibilities. There are so many options available when the canvas is untouched. These potentials are endless, and thus chaotic.

Every decision that the artist makes, beginning with establishing the size and shape of the canvas, limits options and brings order to the disorder. As the artist selects oils, she closes the door on acrylics, watercolors and tempera. Through the myriad decisions that she makes, subtle and coarse, overt and covert, she brings form to the chaos of immeasurable possibilities.

The decisions the artist makes relative to size, shape, form and media are analagously parallel to the internal process of filtering imaginal possibilities. Exactly how this thematic fermentation happens is a mystery.

In *Existential Art Therapy: The Canvas Mirror,* I used the image of a boiling pot of seawater to conceptualize the process. As the water boils and turns to steam it leaves a residue of salt. The salt was always there, but it took the boiling to make it visible. The same thing happens within the psyche of the artist. Feelings, images, themes, conflicts and powerful forces simmer, eventually turning into the artist's "salt," as the artwork is completed.[3]

Making art, whether by professional, amateur, patient, or therapist is a process of structuring chaos. Whatever needs to be expressed will be expressed. Creating art is the process of constantly moving back and forth between order and disorder, spontaneity and composition, chaos and structure.

11. **Art as Hope.** Hope is essential in all forms of psychotherapy. The art therapist must have hope for the patient and the patient must have hope for himself. If there is no hope, there will be little or no therapeutic progress made. It is, of course, to be expected that the patient's hope may be an endangered species. The art therapist's hope then must be solid and unshakeable. Hope requires faith. The patient needs to have faith in the art therapist, the therapist must have faith in the art process, in himself and in the essential goodness and value of all people.

Making art is a symbolic expression of hope. In an unspoken manner engaging in creative activity is an act of generativity; i.e., a giving to the next generation. In order to do this one must believe, at a deep level, that the next generation is worthy of the gift.

I see this principle enacted again and again in the art studio at Harding Hospital. Patients who have been in therapy for awhile subtly welcome and initiate newcomers. The seasoned patient demonstrates to the newly admitted that the Hospital experience can be survived, and in fact, can be good. This happens verbally, behaviorally and symbolically. Patients will often donate one or more of their art pieces to the studio. These are hung on our walls whenever possible. They stimulate the environment, and whether the new patient knew the discharged one or not, there is a powerful message inherent in seeing the gift of someone else's art hanging on the walls. If these paintings could speak I believe they would say to the new patients, "Have faith, hope."

Critical in this hoping is the art therapist's firm conviction that what we do is healthy and curative. Our belief is contagious. Likewise, any doubt we have regarding the integrity of our contribution to the therapy process will infect the air of the studio. Such messages, whether positive or negative, are not a matter of verbalization. They are subtle and covert. This is why it is essential that art therapists remain active artists. It is in the studio that faith in the art making process is nurtured. Creating art is a declaration of faith and hope.

12. **Art as Benevolence.** In art therapy studios patients find their needs met as they give to others. These same patients, in the early stages of therapy, feel empty and barren, as if they have nothing of merit to offer to another human being.

Patients are of tremendous support and help to each other in the studio. They encourage one another, critique one another, share artistic techniques, make suggestions and listen to one another. There are outcome studies that suggest that the relationships among patients that are formed in the context of the treatment situation have as much or more to do with the eventual success or failure of the therapy as do the professional therapists (Huestis & Ryland, 1985).[25-26]

The making of art is an activity of self-transcendence. Patients in a psychiatric hospital are often morosely self-indulgent. Such absorption takes many forms: hopelessness, excessive introspection, and unrelenting self-analysis to name but a few. Yet it is clear, as Viktor Frankl discusses, that meaning can be found only in the context of relationship, and in transcending the self.[4] The doing of art invariably absorbs the patient in a thing outside the self. In the studio this transcendent absorption is a public act. Patients respond to the art work of other patients. There is a contagious benevolence that infects the air of the therapeutic arts studio. Making art is a benevolent act.

These elements delineate disparate aspects of the therapeutic journey. Some of them refer to specific actions or attributes of the process of change, while others might more faithfully be characterized as catalysts or mediums in which transformation occurs. I suspect that these are operative in most therapeutic schemas, but I believe firmly that the art therapy studio is the ideal milieu for their enactment.

This listing of healing elements of the arts in therapy has emerged from my twenty years of clinical experience. It is, to be sure, only a partial inventory of the therapeutic characteristics of art processes. It is not a scientific list verified by statistical study, but it is born of encounters with real live persons who are struggling with their lives. Having observed many patients get better, these are the elements that I find common among them. It is most important that whatever theoretical constructs emerge in our professional writings be based always in the enterprise of helping people feel better.

Chapter XIII

CURATIVE ASPECTS ILLUSTRATED

In this chapter I will discuss again the twelve curative aspects of art therapy. This time however, it is my intent to bring the reader into the art studio and expressive group room in order to give you the feel of these curative aspects at work. I wish that I could convey to you the sounds of these places, the smells, the tastes of the interactions. I have done my best to bring you into the rich and mysterious world of the therapeutic arts work in progress.

The vignettes offered here are by design rather brief. It is my hope that they may point the way for the reader to grasp the concepts of the twelve elements in such a manner as to enable you to identify them at work in all of the other, more lengthy illustrations offered in various segments of this book. Although in other chapters I do not refer directly to these twelve aspects, I believe that you will see their healing effects at work in the vignettes.

In order to make my positions as clear and simple as possible I have sought the wisdom of many experts in this area, i.e., patients that I have known over the past two decades. I have also consulted with graduate students and colleagues in an effort to corroborate my descriptions of what it is that makes doing art a healing process.

Welcome to My World

1. Art As Existentialism

The essence of existential art therapy is found in the visual image. Working from this perspective the art therapist attends to the patient by (1) Doing with them, (2) Being open to them, and (3) Honoring their pain.[3] The primary thrust of the work is engaging the patient in a creative struggle with the ultimate concerns of human existence: death, freedom, isolation, and purpose in life. A central concept in utilizing the arts therapies from an existential base is the notion that the art processes

133

may lead individuals toward a state of mindfulness. A formula regarding this concept is: Artistic expression leads to mindfulness, mindfulness leads to creative anxiety which leads to change/action, which fosters expression which deepens mindfulness. The formula is circular.

Julie's Rocks. When Julie entered the short term treatment unit at Harding Hospital, she was a recent graduate from a prestigious eastern college. Twenty-three years old, intelligent and ambitious but, by her account "chronically depressed." She shared with her primary therapist that she had not felt happy since junior high. "The real lows don't come very often, but I just never feel good."

Julie had been in the expressive art psychotherapy group for two sessions when the images of rocks began to appear. Initially they were seen as part of a tranquil, rather bleak, landscape. Always drawn with black and mottled brown, one was tall and slender, the other roughly circular. They were consistently portrayed as lightly leaning against one another. The rocks recurred over a period of two weeks, though when asked about them Julie would shake her head and say, "I don't have a clue why they are here, they just are."

On one such occasion I shared a thought from James Hillman's, *A Blue Fire,* to the effect that images are necessary angels waiting for a response.[10]

"What do you think he meant by that?" Julie asked.

"Well, I'm not exactly sure how Hillman would answer your question, but I think he's talking about how sometimes images come to us because they have something to say, or something to teach us."

She looked skeptical. "Hmmm. Maybe they are telling me that I should lose some weight." This brought a round of laughter from her peers in the group.

"They do look heavy," I said. "I wonder, if any one in the group was out walking and came upon these rocks, what would your reaction be?"

Bill, a man in his early sixties spoke, "I think they look like a good place to rest. I'd sit on the smaller one and lean back on the tall one."

Jennifer, another recent college graduate chimed in, "I think one is a guy rock and one is a girl."

Marianne, a widow in her mid '30s said, "They look sort of lonely or lost to me. They keep showing up in your drawings, Julie, but it's like they don't know where they belong."

As these words left Marianne's lips Julie's facial expression went from a partial smile to ashen solemnness in a matter of seconds. Sensing the power of the *necessary angels* message I asked Julie if she wanted to say anything more about her drawing.

She shook her head and quietly said, "No."

The next session Julie's rocks again appeared. This time they were depicted as seated on a plush velvet love seat. The room containing them was portrayed as ornate yet cold and uninviting. When it came her turn to speak Julie said, "I've been doing a lot of thinking about these rocks. If they are angels they are mean."

"Julie, sometimes the messages that we most need to hear are the ones we least want to listen to," I said.

"Yes, I know." She replied. "I don't like what the rocks have to say to me." Tears welled in her eyes.

Marianne asked, "What do you think they mean, Julie?"

"I'm not sure, but the other night I was thinking about them and the faces of my mom and dad came into my mind. They were smiling at me and telling me how proud they are of me and what a good daughter I am, and what a great person I am." The tears ran down her cheeks and splattered on her blouse.

Bill said, "That sounds pretty good, Julie. What's the matter with that?"

She sobbed. "It's not true, Bill. It's not true." Through her tears Julie shared with the group that she had gotten pregnant when she was in high school. She and her boyfriend had decided to have an abortion. She had kept both the pregnancy and the abortion a secret from her parents ever since.

Jennifer reached over and placed an arm around Julie's shoulders. "It's alright Jul', It's alright."

"No, no it's not!" She sobbed. "It's all a lie. They think I'm Miss Perfect and I feel horrible. I thought I'd forgotten all about it until those damned rocks showed up."

"Maybe the rocks didn't want things to be forgotten." I said. "Maybe they need the truth to be told. They look pretty solid. I don't think they will crumble."

Julie attended three more expressive group sessions. The rocks came too. The dialogue between them encircled themes of guilt, loneliness, vulnerability and forgiveness. At one point during her final session. Jennifer asked Julie if she was going to tell her parents about the abortion. "I don't know yet," she replied. "But I do know that I have to make a decision about this. I can't just let it slide anymore; the rocks will get in the way."

Nearly four years after Julie left treatment I got a letter from her. She included a photograph of herself and her husband and their infant son. They were standing before a grouping of large rocks along the New England shore line. The letter was, for the most part a newsy one, catching me up on the twists and turns of her life post-hospitalization. She added a P. S. "Everyone knows. The rocks survived."

2. Art as Communication

For many people, whether psychotherapy patient or not, the arts offer an authentic mode of communication that is sorely lacking in their lives. As the individual paints, each line, each shape and each color is a fragment of who he or she is. As the brush moves across the canvas, stories of selfhood are told. Sometimes eloquently, often painfully raw, the tales unfold as images emerge in line, form and color.

David and the Dark. David shuffled into the studio, eyes downcast, hair disheveled. Although it was a typical Ohio February day, damp and cold, he wore his slippers on the walk from the cottage to the creative arts building. He was a tall man, 37 years old, but he looked much older than that. His face was creased with lines which, if read between, told stories of hard times.

I gave him a brief tour of the building and explained that we use the studio as a place to work on important treatment issues creatively. He said, "I can't paint."

It is my experience that often people will share what they most need to share, unconsciously, in the first few moments of therapeutic encounters. Operating from this theory I suggested that I could teach him how to paint. He shook his head but seemed to lack the energy to resist more vociferously. The rest of that first session was spent in building the frame, stretching and gessoing the canvas.

The next day David and I began to talk about possible themes for his first painting. He said that he had no idea what to do.

I asked, "If you tried to describe the way you've been feeling, what sort of words would you use?"

"They tell me that I'm depressed." He sighed.

"David," I replied. "I'm not interested in what anyone else has told you about how you feel. How would you describe yourself?"

He thought for a moment. "Dark." He said.

"Like the night, or like in a cave?" I inquired.

"It's like being in a woods at night. I can't run and I can't see."

"Yowsa! What a great image." I exclaimed. "How about we paint your night woods?"

"I told you before, Bruce, I can't paint. I don't know where I'd begin."

"Trust me," I said. "I think you should start by mixing up some midnight blue. We'll need a lot of it."

"How do I do that?"

I gathered together jars of ultramarine blue, raw umber, black, and cobalt blue and told David to experiment on a piece of palette paper. I also gave him a container and told him that when he'd gotten the color he wanted to use he should mix enough to fill it.

About fifteen minutes later David approached me with a full container of deep blue. "Now what?"

"Step one David is cover your entire canvas with the dark."

"The whole thing?"

"The whole thing," I replied. "You see, I think it's best to get rid of the white emptiness as soon as possible."

When that was completed we began to talk about a path, and trees, and rocks that he imagined would be in the woods. (I thought it encouraging that his first image was of a path. This suggested a preconscious sense of hope and direction.)

Using the midnight blue as a base color David added burnt sienna and arrived at the shade he wanted for the path. From there he went on to alter his dark blue with burnt umber for tree trunks, hooker green and a touch of white for leaves and grays for rocks.

David's handling of color became the object of much conversation in the studio. Fellow patients and therapists alike would stop and comment on his subtle variations on dark blue. The painting grew into a fine study of dim shapes half hidden by the somber and haunting night air of the forest. If one observed the painting from 15 feet away it appeared to be nothing more than shadows. At closer range, however, the observer was presented with a multitude of fine details.

As David worked he shared with me that he used to love to make car models, and that his favorite part of that process was painting the particulars. "You know," he said, "I'd forgotten about that. It's been so long."

I knew from reading his medical chart that David had been married, but that his wife had died in childbirth. The baby, a daughter, had died too. That had been about five years before he came to treatment. In that time he had resigned from his job as an insurance salesman, withdrawn from his family, lost his house and eventually most of his friends.

David's chart also indicated that there was concern on the part of the treatment team that he was talking to noone on the unit, and that he avoided going to see his psychotherapist. Although he had ample insurance resources, it was feared that if he did not begin to engage more actively his coverage would be denied.

As the painting neared completion he began to express concern that it was, "Too dark."

"Well David, I'm not so sure. In fact I've been wondering if you shouldn't try to make it darker."

"I don't understand, Bruce. Why do you say that?"

"It seems to me that you are interested in everything in your life staying as cheerless as possible. I just thought that maybe you might want to darken some of these areas on your painting."

In a somewhat exasperated tone David said, "But I just told you that I was thinking about trying to make it lighter. Now you say make it darker. That doesn't make any sense at all."

"David, I think that when we create things we are making self-portraits. If you add light to this forest I think that you'll have to see what is there more clearly."

"So? What's your point?"

"My point David, is that if you start to be able to see in the darkness of your woods, you'll also have to start to see in the gloom of your life."

He sat back thoughtfully. "Bruce, when Susan and the baby died I thought I never wanted to see another good thing ever again. It really has been like this woods—dark, and frightening and lonely. I don't know why, but I just got tired of talking about it with people, or they got tired of hearing about my misery. I just shut down. Somehow, and I don't understand it, doing this painting has made all that clear to me. People have said so many nice things about this place. (He gently extended his hand and touched the canvas.) It's made me want to see more. Will you teach me how to make moonlight? I want it to be on the tree limbs and the grass."

I gave David a brief lesson in light and shadow. He did the rest.

The painting gave David an opportunity to express the grief and anguish that he had run out of words to express. With each motion of the brush, each dip into the midnight blue, he told his tale of loneliness and sorrow. The imaging of the story allowed him to move beyond its confines. The creative act allowed him to reclaim his right to author his own life. He no longer surrenders to the twist of fate that had ensnared him. His darkness has light and his life goes on.

3. Art as Soul

I embrace the belief that art images come from the depths of human experiences. Born of passion, conflict and creative disquiet, art processes make meaning visible by elevating random events to the realm of potent experiences. The truly extraordinary gift of the art therapist to the clinical setting is our capacity to facilitate the art/soul making process. It is in the moments of our lives when aimless events are turned into meaning-filled experiences that soul is most present. The process of making art is a *process of ensoulment.* This is work that only art therapists can do. It is a sacred task.

Linda Red and Black. Linda wouldn't speak. It was not that she could not, she would not. She was the victim of years of sexual and physical abuse and emotional neglect. It was as if she had just run out of words to say. She would not speak.

When she was referred to the expressive art psychotherapy group I wondered how it would be for her. During the first session, as I explained the group structure to her, Linda made fleeting eye contact with me, but quickly averted her gaze. "Linda, this is a group where we use drawing as a way of getting in touch with, and sharing, feelings. You don't have to be Picasso or anybody like that. Whatever you do will be ok. The only other thing that I ask is that when someone else is speaking we all pay attention. I believe that everybody in this group has a long history of people not taking their feelings seriously. In this group we will always take your feelings seriously. Welcome to the group, I'm glad you are with us."

One of the patients from Linda's living unit said, "I don't think that talking out of turn will be a problem for Linda." In a gentle and accepting way the other members of the group chuckled.

The beginning ritual of this group is to sit in a circle and briefly share the feeling that each member is entering the group with that day. As it came Linda's turn she held her arms tightly against her body, wrapping herself in a defensive cocoon. She rocked forward in her chair, but said nothing. (In a sense her posture and motion explained clearly the feelings of vulnerability and anxiety that she felt. No words were really necessary.)

Addressing the group I said, "Today, I want us to imagine a place that is safe. When the image comes, try to draw what you see."

We work with vividly colored poster chalks on large sheets (3' × 3') of brown craft paper that are hung on the wall with masking tape. Without hesitation Linda moved to a place at the wall and began to draw. She covered the paper quickly with solid red. She then used black to sketch a primitive rendition of a closet. The closet had a steeply slanted ceiling, a slatted door, and a pole with empty hangers dangling from it. In one corner a huddled figure curled against the walls. When it came time to discuss her image Linda shook her head and huddled in much the same position as the figure in the drawing.

In many ways this first session represents the entirety of Linda's therapeutic art journey. She eventually did say a few words, but never more than four or five in one session. Rather she portrayed places, people, and happenings from her life—images in red and black. Sometimes the scenes were frightening to me, sometimes disturbing, sometimes too mysterious for me to comprehend. By making images of these places and events Linda ensouled them. She took time and gave attention to people and space through her creative work. Often her image-people were the ones who had treated her so inhumanely; the places were the scenes of the crimes against her. Yet, they were also more than that, for Linda used her *capacity to make* to place herself in the position of the creator. By doing so she ennobled her position and shifted from that of the victim, to that of the heroine.

On one particularly remarkable day Linda drew a fierce black panther about to pounce upon a small, quivering child, as if to devour it. One of her peers in the group reacted, "Oh Linda, you poor thing. That beast is going to kill you."

Linda turned to her friend and replied, "I'm panther."

Her two-word sentence led the group into an intense discussion of our inner animal nature. When the group was wrapping up I asked Linda, "What are you leaving with today?"

Linda roared.

In the sanctuary of the studio, and the expressive group therapy room, soul is made as imaged confessions, thanksgivings, pleas and praises are *arted out.* The making of images opens us to the mystery that is within each person, patient and therapist alike. It is a sacred thing to look through the soul windows of another.

There are those in the art therapy profession who would say that since Linda did not validate verbally my imaginings about her pictures, my discussion of her work as ensouling is hogwash. They would argue that progress, in Linda's case, is not measurable nor scientifically verifiable, ergo non-existent.

To such colleagues I must respond with all due respect, I was there. I saw her transform from a silent, frightened shell of a person, to a quietly strong and whole woman. I saw Linda get well.

Making art is making soul. Linda was able to discover meaning in the awful and senseless events of her past. She created an imaginative portrait of herself from a new perspective, that of the panther. With each new drawing she anchored herself to the artistic foundation of life, thereby giving herself the strength and courage required to embrace the depth, passion, and conflict of her inner world. She did so almost exclusively through images. She had no need of words.

4. Art as Mastery

As art therapists we must maintain a profound respect for the work, the mastery, of art processes and products. We must approach all aspects of our task with reverence. The patient, the image, the procedures and the quality of craftsmanship all must be embraced fully by artist therapists. Mastery of materials and the techniques of handling them promotes a sense of inner adequacy which is intrinsically therapeutic. Mastery of process and media is linked inextricably to self-discipline, which is likewise bound to self-regard. When one approaches artistic work from a perspective that values quality equally with expressive content, an apperception of sacred passion in the work is revealed. From this springs a new and enriched view of one's life itself. Sacred passion is exposed in authentic, vital and creative interactions between the self and the world. The artist's engagement with media and process is such an interaction.

In the deepest sense, mastery may be described as the capacity to organize raw materials and events, work creatively with them, and transform them into objects and meaningful experiences.

A Bottle, A Cup and a Box of Tissues. Ronnie's early work in the studio resembled colorful vomit. His style of using materials and tools was also reminiscent of regurgitation. He poured huge amounts of paint directly onto un-gessoed masonite boards. He refused to invest the time that gessoing would entail, and he was, "Not about to fart around building something that ain't even going to show when I'm done" (stretcher frame).

Initially my colleagues in the creative arts studio encouraged Ronnie's efforts. They saw his work as cathartic and immediately expressive. I had a rather different reaction, however. I saw his handling of the paint as excessive and wasteful. His refusal to go through the proper procedural steps of building a canvas, or gessoing the masonite panels, as resistive and defensive. He often left paint-filled brushes unwashed in the sink. Had I not attended to them they would have been ruined.

After some time had passed with no notable change in Ronnie's engagement in the studio, and no discernible reshaping of his interactive style which was responsible for his being hospitalized, I suggested to my peers that we were spinning our wheels with Ronnie. One of my colleagues irritably exhorted me to take the clinical responsibility for Ronnie. After some thoughtful discussion I agreed to do so.

SESSION 1.

"Ronnie, I'm going to be working with you for awhile out here in the studio."

"I don't need any help."

"I'm not sure that I agree with you, Ron. But whether we agree or not, I have been assigned to work with you."

He went about his task of gathering paint containers and brushes.

I said. "You won't be needing that stuff today, Ron. You see I've been thinking about you a lot. I think you might have some good skills, but you don't seem to be able to use them very effectively."

He looked at me with a mixture of irritation and curiosity. "What the hell are you talkin' about?"

"I haven't kept an exact count, but I think that you've done about 7 or 8 paintings since you've been here. None of them are very well thought out, and technically you've made a lot of mistakes."

"Who gives a . . . ?"

"I do, Ronnie." I interrupted. "It's sort of like if I took you to the piano in the Campus Center and told you to just play. You could bang on the keys, you might make a lot of noise, you might even be able to convey some kind of feeling. But you would not be able to make music."

He stared at me wide eyed. "So you think my paintings are like noise."

"Yes," I said. "They are ok for beginner's noise. But they are not the music that you could make. So let's put the paints away and start to work."

Reluctantly he did so. "Now what?" He asked.

I gave him a 12 × 18 sheet of white drawing paper and a #2 lead pencil. "We are going to start by learning to draw perspective. First I need you to decide where the horizon line should be."

And so Ronnie's lessons in mastery began. He learned to do one-, two- and three-point perspective drawing. He did them and did them and did them again. Then I shifted his attention to mastering the basic shapes: squares, rectangles, circles, ovals, triangles, cylinders, cones and spheres. From there we moved on to learning to shade, not with the side of the pencil, but with the point and a gentle touch. I often told him to, "Use the six P's: Prior Planning and Patience Provides for a Positive Performance. He learned.

After these elemental steps were mastered I placed a green bottle, plastic cup, and a box of facial tissues on the table before him. "Draw these," I said.

He began immediately, and confidently, to draw the shapes that were before him.

The look on his face as he completed this drawing was a mixture of awe and pride. His peers in the studio were quick to praise his efforts and the pleasure this brought Ronnie was obvious to even the most casual observer.

Ronnie got better while hospitalized, not through cathartic expressive processes, but by learning to struggle with quality in his work. In an artistic sense we lived out the attention to quality that is described in *Zen and the Art of Motorcycle Maintenance.* [27]

Art therapists must take seriously the quality of our patient's work. We must not delude ourselves by thinking that expression is the only end of the arts in therapy. At every juncture we must encourage patients not only to exorcise haunting emotions, but to develop artistic skills as well. Often patients initially want to view the creative arts studio as a metaphoric garbage dump for feelings they long to discard. My insistence that attention be paid to mastery and quality is anchored in the belief that *mastery* and *care* are synonymous. My investment in their lives and their wellbeing is manifest in my interest in their creations. I have no expectation that my patients will become great artists. I do expect them to learn to take care in their work, which will in turn instruct them in caring about quality in their own lives.

5. Art as Personal Metaphor

An extraordinary aspect of the position of the art therapist is our capacity to see and respond to the visual and action metaphors of our patients. I believe that all things we create are partial self-portraits. It is critical that art therapists honor the communications that are presented in patient imagery. As a profession, we must be committed to the premise that images can, and should, just be. They must be regarded as having lives of their own. We should not allow them to be dissected or "imaginally" autopsied.

If images are regarded as living metaphors, this promotes a reverent approach by those seeking to be in dialogue with them. The notion of dialogue,[23] precludes the injurious and unethical phenomenon of imagicide.[3]

Kerry and the Dog. When Kerry came to the hospital she was twenty-one years old, an over-indulged, unemancipated college student who experienced severe panic attacks, particularly whenever her parents planned to be away from home. Kerry's father was a very successful business man who regularly travelled and often asked his wife to accompany him. These ventures were recurrently disrupted by some outrageous and self-defeating behavior on Kerry's part. In the months prior to her hospitalization Kerry's actions had become increasingly dramatic and destructive. On one occasion she drank alcohol to excess, took a handfull of aspirin, and drove her late model sports car into a tree. She was lucky to be alive.

As Kerry participated in the expressive art psychotherapy group I found myself vaguely angry at her rather obnoxious and socially oblivious manner. She was a snob. She denied that her parents had anything to do with her difficulties, and she was stubborn and immature.

Somewhere along the way, however, I began to really listen to the stories she told as she described her drawings. During one session it struck me that the reason her struggle with emancipation aroused such irritation in me was that it recalled my own feelings of abandonment and fear as I had lived through my own separation process. Though her wealthy, over-giving parents were very different from mine, the feelings were not. How dare she make me remember?

An image that Kerry often drew, was of a disheveled dog. Whenever she was asked about this image she would shrug her shoulders and say that it was just something that she liked to draw. Rather than push her for a cognitive explanation of this recurrent image, I decided to create an imaginal dialogue with it. I began the next session by telling this story.

Outside a certain town, at a certain time, not too long ago a man was traveling by car when he ran out of gas. As he walked through the countryside toward the next town he came upon a dreadful sight. Beside a rundown old shack there was a rundown old dog house. In front of the dog house lay an old mongrel licking an open wound on his side. One of his eyes was swollen shut and his hide looked as if it had been years since he'd been bathed. The man was moved with pity and he approached the animal. The closer he got, he saw even more evidence of mistreatment. The traveller was appalled.

He said, "Oh you poor thing."

Since this was a magical land the dog raised his head and said, "Are you talking to me?"

"Yes," the man replied. "Yes, my God, how did you get to be such a mess?"

Without hesitating the dog said, "It's my master. He has many stresses in his life. When he comes home from his work he beats me."

The man felt even more compassion. "Well, why do you stay here? Your tether is rotted. Surely you could run away."

The dog blinked his good eye and said, "But he always feeds me so well."

I then asked the group to draw their responses to the story. Kerry's image was full of rage at the dog's master. As we talked about the drawings Kerry blurted out, "All I have to say is that the food must be pretty damned good!"

Another patient in the group turned to Kerry and asked, "Well, how good is it, Kerry?" She fumed momentarily and then began a mixed laughing/crying session. She had discovered the meaning of her recurrent drawings of the disheveled puppy.

Intuitively, and unconsciously the image of the dog had been trying to get the message to Kerry that it was time to grow up, even if growing up meant not always being as well fed as she had been accustomed to.

Kerry did not immediately change her life as a result of her images and my imaginal response to them, but she did cease to resist dealing with the role that her relationship with her parents played in her self-defeating behaviors.

By responding to her metaphor with a metaphor of my own, I helped Kerry to see herself in the mirror of her drawings. I do not mean to imply that this was all there was to Kerry, nor was there only one meaning to be found in her image of the dog. There was much more to her than her dependence, as there was more to the dog than hunger.

In this interchange I did not make an interpretation, rather I engaged in imaginal dialogue that allowed Kerry to participate with the metaphor. I believe that had I attempted to make a literal, or clever, analysis of drawings she would have withdrawn from me and the group. She would not have been helped in the slightest. Conversely, I think that any interpretive dissection on my part would have served to kill the image messenger, and injure the patient artist.

6. Art as Empowerment

To empower means to give official authority or legal power to, or to enable.[13] The person seeking therapy often feels a deep sense of having been disempowered. He frequently views himself as the victim of those who have more power than he does. Family, friends and the world are experienced as hostile and disenfranchising.

In order to combat a disempowered stance words are not enough. Empowerment is not a process that can be enacted through language alone. There must be experiences that promote the reclamation of power within the individual. Acts of empowerment are processes of transformation from the position of the victim, to that of the heroine, and from a passive response to the world to an active engagement with it.

Art therapists do not attempt to do away with the struggles of our patients, rather we seek to enable them to find meaning in their efforts. The empowering nature of art therapy is found in its capacity to accept and embrace distress, not in its desire to rid the patient of it. The arts bring our deepest fears, loneliness, and anguish to our attention. Rather than "cure" these discomforting aspects of life art therapy enables persons to live with them courageously and with meaning.

Sharon and the Sea. Sharon had heard about art therapy, and my private practice, from a friend. She told me during our first telephone contact that she felt "a little funny," about calling a therapist of any kind. When I inquired as to what she meant, she explained that she wasn't sure that her problems really required any professional help. "Maybe I'm just feeling sorry for myself," she sighed. After several minutes on the phone she said that she wanted to come into the office to meet me, but that she was making no commitment to "really be in therapy." I assured her that whatever she decided would be fine and that I was willing to meet with her in order to give her time to make up her mind.

My colleague and office-mate, John Reece, has discussed with me the theory that patients seeking therapy often lay out the entire course of their work in the first five minutes of the therapeutic encounter. The rest of the time, John asserts, is spent in the patient and therapist attempting to make sense out of what was communicated in those first five minutes. I am in no position to embrace this as a universal tenet, but it was certainly the case in relation to Sharon.

The difficulties of Sharon's life, that she felt a little funny about seeking therapy for, included the recent death of her husband, unresolved feelings of anger toward her father who had been a distant and demanding figure, and her son's departure from the home for college.

When Sharon arrived at my office the next week I was immediately struck by my positive first impressions of her. While I would not describe myself as overly cautious in new relationships, I would say that I tend to take my time warming up to people. Sharon, though, had an instant positive impact upon me. She looked to be in her late forties or early fifties. A tall woman of medium build, she carried herself well. As she introduced herself to me she established and held eye contact easily. There was a sadness in her eyes and I sensed that this was a new experience for her. It was not that her life had been a fairy-tale, but that she had always been surrounded with people who could support her through her life's struggles. Now she found herself facing profound losses and no shoulder to cry on.

Sharon: "I'm still not exactly sure why I am here, Mr. Moon."

Bruce: "I don't know exactly why you've come to me either, Sharon. You did say on the phone that a friend had told you about me. Is that right?"

Sharon: "Yes."

Bruce: "Let's start there. What did your friend tell you?"

Sharon: "She said that you had helped her daughter a few years ago when she was a teen-ager."

Bruce: "Something about what she said must have sounded appealing."

Sharon: "I think it was that she told me that you and her daughter would paint pictures together."

Bruce: "You'd like to learn to paint?"

Sharon: "Yes, I've always wanted to, but I never took the time."

Bruce: "You have a lot of time now?"

Sharon: "Yes, too much time." As these words were spoken her eyes brimmed with tears. We sat in silence for a few moments. "My husband, Tom, and I were planning to go to Hilton Head

Island this spring. We were there once, a long time ago. We always said we'd get back there . . . but we were so busy."

Bruce: Sensing the poignancy and richness of this revelation I said, "We could paint the sea, if you decide to get into treatment."

Sharon: "I wouldn't know where to begin."

Bruce: "I know how to start, but you would have to help me."

Sharon: "How could I help you?"

Bruce: "You'd have to be able to describe the place that you want to paint in great detail."

Sharon: "Oh, I could do that, all right."

This is how Sharon entered into the art therapy journey. She was struggling with a deep feelings of loss and loneliness. Yet, she was still interested in her life. She did not seem overtly bitter or angry about her situation, just rather overwhelmed by it. By the end of that first half hour interview I was sure that I wanted to be helpful to Sharon. I was also confident that engaging in art processes would be very beneficial for her. She agreed, and we decided to begin meeting on a weekly basis for one hour.

She began to tell me stories about the sea. She painted and shared night walks on the beach, wind storms, and skinny dipping on a lonely stretch of shoreline south of Kitty Hawk, North Carolina.

I would respond to her by demonstrating wash and overlay techniques, suggesting that a touch more white be added to the ultramarine, and helping her with light glints on her waves.

Sharon completed three paintings while in therapy. The first portrays her and Tom huddled against the wind as a stormy sea crashes against a rocky shoreline. The second depicts them sitting side by side gazing at a sunset over calm water. In the third painting Sharon stands, facing the horizon alone. The sea is rough but not overwhelming and the sky is clear.

Through the making of these three images Sharon ennobled her struggle with letting go of her husband and getting on with her life. She transformed the pain into images. She did not make the pain go away, rather she accepted it. Sharon was able to stop being controlled by her feelings of loneliness and abandonment and was able to use them as the source of her creative work. This enabled her to live courageously in the presence of her loss. The paintings provide a metaverbal chronicle of her therapeutic journey. Moving from the position of the clinging person caught in a storm, to that of a loving wife recalling quiet moments with her husband. Finally, the third painting portrays a woman standing alone, in full daylight. The sea is not calm, nor is it overpowering; the natural turmoil of this phase of Sharon's life was dramatically represented.

As she discovered the artistic power of painting over, reworking and changing direction with her paintings, Sharon also embraced her power over her own existence.

7. Art as Work

The making of art is neither easy nor comfortable. Being in therapy is likewise neither easy nor comfortable. The labors of artists and psychotherapy patients are marked by sore muscles, blistered hands and hearts. Art is work.

... To be sure, all of this is done in order to create something for which reason we can call it work and not rage.[28]

Patients come to art therapy in order to involve themselves in the creative work of transforming destructive energy into constructive ends. They come to work out potent intra- and interpersonal conflicts. This is neither easy nor comfortable, it is hard work.

The sense of mastery derived from creative *work* is integrally connected to the development of self-discipline, which is ultimately connected to pleasure. From artistic work grows a sacred passion for life as it is. This sacred passion is marked by authentic, creative and vital involvement with materials, the self and others. Engaging in art tasks establishes a therapeutic milieu in which destructive forces are transformed into meaningful objects. Making art is a process of organizing the millions of imaginal possibilities that swirl in a chaotic mass of potential. Psychotherapy is a process of organizing the turbulent and chaotic inner feelings, sensations, conflicts and behaviors that are the signposts of emotional distress. This is hard work.

Allen, I See What You Have Made. Allen was in his late thirties when I first met him. He came to the hospital after a series of bizarre acts that had resulted in his being arrested on two occasions. He had been threatened with detention by the police after several other incidents of strange behaviors. He was a tall and gangly man with deep-set eyes encased by dark circles. He dressed in a sloppy manner and exhibited poor personal hygiene habits. His teeth were yellowed, as were the tips of his fingers on his left hand, from chain smoking unfiltered cigarettes. He seldom spoke to the treatment staff or his fellow patients.

He was diagnosed as having a chronic schizophrenic disorder with paranoid features. The early impression of the psychiatry resident assigned to be Allen's medical manager was that his hospital stay would be relatively brief with the primary goal being to stabilize him on psychotropic medications and return him to his marginal level of functioning at home. The psychiatrist supervising the young resident was confident that Allen would benefit little from anything other than psychopharmacology. He echoed his student's view that Allen's condition was not hopeful and that perhaps the best the treatment team could do was contain his disturbing acting-out behaviors until the medicine kicked in.

Despite this rather limited plan and dismal prognosis, the resident did not object to Allen's being placed in a full regimen of therapeutic activities which included: studio art, greenhouse, and leisure sports. The head nurse on the unit expressed some concern that, "he won't really do what you want him to and you people will have to watch him like a hawk."

Early in his involvement in the arts studio Allen was asked to do a variety of creative activities: painting, drawing and collage making. Although he was cooperative and seemed to make a genuine effort, his productions were crude and poorly executed. He remained non-communicative.

One morning the art therapy staff was very busy due to an influx of new patients who needed to be oriented to the building and the activities that we do there. Allen stood quietly by the sink, seeming to be in his own world. No one paid much attention to him until one of my colleagues noticed that Allen had bent a coffee can, that had served as a water container. The therapist began to confront him about abusing materials. I sensed that Allen's bending was neither malicious or random. He was attempting to shape the brightly colored metal. I intervened and asked Allen to follow me to the tool cabinet where I gave him a pair of metal shears and needle nosed pliers. Without really looking at me he said, "Thank you."

He then began to work, shaping, cutting and bending the coffee can into the form of a whimsical bird. As the session neared its end he approached me and asked, "Thread?"

"Sure, Allen, what color would you like?"

"Yellow."

He attached a three-foot piece of thread to the body of the bird, then hung it from a nail above a doorway. As someone moved under it the wind of the passer-by gently nudged the bird. It appeared to float in the air. Allen smiled.

It seemed clear to me that the initial attempts to involve Allen in two-dimensional creative acts had missed the mark, while three-dimensional work engaged him. Working from this hypothesis I introduced him to a form of stone sculpture.

In our setting it is not possible to work with traditional stone sculpture materials. The process is too time consuming and cost-prohibitive. We have, however, arrived at an acceptable solution. We make our own stone by blending concrete mix and vermiculite. By varying the amount of vermiculite added to the mixture, the hardness and resistiveness of the material can be altered. The more vermiculite, the softer the block.

The average block of stone that we made at that time was about two cubic feet. Allen fell in love with this material and the tools used to shape it. He hammered and chiseled, filed and sanded, piece after piece. As the chips fell away graceful shapes emerged. Abstract masses that were both energetic and elegant hinted at animal forms. Allen's hammer and chisel breathed life into the inanimate gray concrete.

This was not an easy enterprise. As his confidence and skill level grew he asked for increasingly harder stones to work with. These allowed for finer and more detailed pieces. It was hard work. His hands blistered and he sweat. His muscles strained as he pounded, smoothed and gouged the stone.

To be sure, all of this was done in order to create something, for which reason we can call it work and not rage. [28]

Allen did not cease to be a schizophrenic as a result of his involvement with hammer, chisel, stone and me. But he did create several intriguing and graceful images from hunks of gray concrete and vermiculite. More important, we established a comraderie that was altogether different from the isolated and detached stance he had maintained before he came to the hospital. Did his engagement with coffee cans and stone take away his paranoid ideation? No. Did his consistent attendance to the creative arts session, once daily, five days a week, improve his personal hygiene or his socialization skills? No, not really. So, what was the point of his being in art therapy at all?

In the time he spent in the hospital Allen made a dozen or so sculptures. He let people watch him as he worked. Sometimes he would respond when they asked a question. Sometimes his face lit up as he watched another human being touch the smooth edge of one of his works. I believe that Allen made contact with the world in a way that he had never done before. There are no psychological measuring sticks to quantify the qualitative difference that creating art made in Allen's life. Measurable or not, there was a difference that could be felt more than seen. When I last heard from him he wrote that he had switched to wood carving. He said that it was a lot easier to clean up the mess.

I do not know if Allen has become any more functional in the practical sense of the word, but I have faith that both his inner world, and the larger community has been enriched by his artistic work.

8. Art as Play

Artistic play makes a dynamic source of energy available to us. An inherent aspect of art is that it brings pleasure, allowing us to contend with and take part in life. The arts promote a sensual relationship with the environment.

The sculptor feels the impact of chisel against stone. The dancer feels the weight of his body through his feet. The ceramicist feels the slippery ooze of wet clay spinning between her hands on the potters wheel. The painter smells the linseed oil and senses the roughness of the canvas as brush pushes pigment across the surface. The processes of making art demand that artists touch the world.

There is an imaginal mysterious quality to art that allows emotions, fantasies and wishes into our daily lives. The arts evoke and intensify feelings while at the same time providing a safe structure for their expression which is often fun. The infusion of the magical and imaginal enlivens the familiar and routine.

Sandy's **Dance.** Sandy had been admitted to the hospital the afternoon before she was referred to the Expressive Art Therapy Group. When she entered the group room she moved slowly, as if carrying a heavy weight. I introduced her to the other members and explained that this was a group where we used drawing as a way of getting in touch with, and sharing, feelings. I asked her if she had ever tried to draw her feelings before.

Sandy: No, I haven't drawn anything since I left elementary school.

Bruce: Well, that's good, this'll really be something new and different for you.

Sandy: Why did they want me to be here? It sounds a little childish to me.

Bruce: I suppose some people might think that it is silly. But, I think it's a good thing to express your feelings and using art can be a fun way to do it.

Sandy: So, what are we supposed to do?

Bruce: In a minute I'll give the group a theme to draw about then we'll draw for awhile. When we're done we'll spend some time talking about the pictures. At the end of the session we'll take the drawings down off the wall and you can either take yours with you, or throw it away.

Sandy grimaced.

What's the point of doing it if you are just going to throw it away.

Bruce: You can keep your drawings if you want to, Sandy, but that's not the point.

Another group member said, "You'll get used to it. It is a little embarrassing at first, but Bruce always says 'trust the process,' and it can really feel good, sometimes.

Bruce: Today, as a way of getting warmed up I'd like us to close our eyes. Imagine yourself dancing. Now keeping your eyes closed get a piece of chalk in both hands and move against your paper. Let your hands make the dance.

There were some mild groans of protest but I could tell by the chalk noises in the room that everyone was doing what I'd asked them to do. After a few minutes I told the group that they could open their eyes and look around at the dances on the wall.

Sandy's dance was drawn in sky blue and white. The image had a light, delicate and airy feel to it. I commented that it reminded me of a ballet.

Sandy: When I was a little girl I used to imagine that someday I would be a famous dancer. My brother used to make platform stages for me out of cardboard and I would dance and dance and dance.

Bruce: Your image seems very light and fanciful.

Sandy: There was a song, I think Judy Collins sang it. It was about a girl whose father always promised her someday they would live in France, and that she could learn to dance. I loved that song.

(Sandy, at this point was both smiling and gently crying.)

My father always promised us
that we would live in France.
He'd go boating on the Seine
And I could learn to dance.

We lived in Ohio then,
he worked in the mines... [29]

Bruce: Yes, I know the song. It is beautiful, like your image.
Sandy: I haven't thought of that game with my brother in twenty years.
Bruce: It's a good memory?
Sandy: It is good, but I feel sad, thinking about it.
Bruce: What is it that stirs the sadness?
Sandy: It's been so long since I felt that way. Free, able to dance. (She looked down at the floor.) I don't know, I can't even remember the last time I felt good about anything.
Bruce: Your drawing is very nice, Sandy.
Sandy: May I keep it?
Bruce: It is yours.

There is tremendous therapeutic value inherent in the process of making art. There are fleeting qualities of perception, elusive bits of light and shadow, sound and physical sensations captured as the patient/ artist moves across the page, chalk in hand.

Play: to move swiftly, to touch lightly, to flutter and vibrate, contend with and take part. To move freely, especially within prescribed limits... to bring about work and to keep in action... [12]

As Sandy's brief hospitalization unfolded it was fascinating to watch her regain her *life force.* Both in the expressive group, and in the fine arts studio Sandy rediscovered her capacity to play. Artistic play reacquainted her with her dynamic internal energy. This was evident as she dealt with the past and as she experimented with her imagination in the present.

9. Art as Relationship

Meaning can be found only in the context of relationship to others. In order for life to have purpose, the individual self must be transcended.

The making of art is a transcendent act. In nearly every instance, the artist is interested in the reaction his, or her, work will inspire in others. This interest is essentially motivated by the longing for contact with others.

There are no significant psychotherapeutic systems that are not focused on interpersonal relationships. Art therapy is no exception. A central theme of our work is promoting relationship, both in our approach to the patient and his art, and in our therapeutic goals and objectives. Although many artists are professedly private, most artists aim their creative work toward other people. Making art is thus a process concerned with community, with deepening relationships.

The community of the expressive arts psychotherapy groups that I lead have invested me with a level of authority to work with the imaged burdens my patients bring. They cast them upon the walls of the studio. Through the rituals of creation we engage in a process of acknowledgment of the way our lives are. The deepest intent of arting out the painful pieces of self is to empower patients to grasp the full meaning of their images. This is most profoundly done in the company of others.

Michelle's Hands. The drawing seemed innocuous enough. Michelle had used black and white chalk on brown paper to depict two hands clutching a metal bar.

The group, consisting of six severely disturbed adolescent girls, had been a wild one. One of the girls had come to the session directly from special care (seclusion) where she'd spent the night before in restraints. Another was all wound up, in anticipation of her first family therapy session. She'd been on "therapeutic separation" for three weeks. The other four were, in varying degrees, angry, depressed and resistive. It was one of those days when I felt I'd earned my salary just by containing the affect of the group.

So, Michelle's low key drawing had not grabbed much attention. As it came her turn to share her drawing with the group she said quietly, "When I drew this I wasn't sure I'd say anything about it to you. This is hard for me to look at."

"You don't have to say anything, Michelle."

"I know," she replied. "I'm not deaf, Bruce. I've heard you say that crap about a thousand times."

"I just want you to know that I think it's most important that you do the art. Talking's OK, but it's not the main thing in this group."

"I know. Now will you let me to this?" She paused. "This is a picture of my hands. They are holding on to the railing of the bed I used to sleep in when I was a little girl." She began to cry, the room became still. "I used to hold onto the rail so tight. I was so afraid." More tears. One of her peers in the group moved her chair closer to Michelle's.

I stood and got the box of tissues from the counter and laid it beside Michelle's chair.

"My dad used to get drunk and come into my room. I had to hold onto the rail or else I was afraid I'd hit him or hurt him. He'd . . . you know . . . I loved him. Oh God, it makes me want to puke."

"You've been through a lot, Michelle."

Silence.

Speaking to the group I said, "You know, there are days in this group that I am awed by what happens here. What an honor it is for me to be with you all sometimes."

Michelle said, "This hurts so fucking bad."

"Michelle, I believe that things we draw are sort of like self-portraits. I also believe that you can change the picture, if that's what you want to do."

She looked at me skeptically. "What are you talking about?

"You can change the image, Michelle. You aren't that little girl anymore. You can let go of the rail, you can draw fists, lock your bedroom door, anything you want."

"No, I want to keep this one the way it is. But I think I'll draw some more pictures like this."

Beth, another girl in the group said, "Well, if I was you I'd tear that damned thing off the wall."

"No, I just want to roll it up and keep it." She stood and with great ceremony tightly rolled the paper into a tight cylinder.

In the sessions that followed many scenes of Michelle's hands were drawn. They gradually let go of the bed rail. She gave them color, balled them into fists and pounded them against to image of her father. In one of her later works she opened them, as if in a gesture of offering. With the support of her peers in the group she moved from images of tight constriction, to rage, to consolation.

If, as I have suggested earlier, art making is soul making, then we art therapists are essentially shepherds of souls. We guide our patients and clients as best we can toward that which will nourish them. We watch out for danger, retrieve those who are lost and help to sustain the wounded. We do not send them out alone. We accompany.

10. Art, Structure and Chaos

As the artist stands before the untouched drawing pad or sits before the uncentered clay spinning on the potter's wheel the possibilities are infinite. All decisions she makes bring order and limits to the chaotic potential of the work not started.

In the world of the artist, chaos demands process, which leads to structure, yielding product. In the world of the disturbed psychiatric patient, chaos demands process, which leads to structure, yielding engagement in life.

Richard. During Richard's initial interview with an adjunctive therapist he fell asleep. He was nine years old. He suffered from Attention Deficit Hyperactive Disorder, Major Depression and Adjustment Reaction/ Severe.

Richard was abandoned by his biological parents when he was two months old. Since then he'd been in a host of foster care and residential care settings. He had also been adopted, at age six, only to be de-adopted at eight.

He told the adjunctive therapist that he had no hobbies, no interests, and no curiosity about the activity therapy program. The therapist had very little information to go on in terms of designing a therapeutic schedule for Richard. She decided that she would try to meet with him again the following day.

The next day, when she arrived at the unit, Richard was in seclusion. Two days later she again approached him about his therapeutic activity schedule. This time Richard was very distracted, suspicious. His attention span was very short.

The adjunctive therapist decided to schedule Richard into Greenhouse activity, physical education/recreation, and communication skills group. Within the first few hours Richard had been sent back to the unit from each activity area. He swore, spit and kicked.

In Physical Education, his explosive behaviors constantly got him involved in altercations with his peers and the therapists. In Greenhouse he isolated and did things, "my way or not at all." In communications skills he manifested a variety of bizarre behaviors which set him apart from his peers and reinforced his negative self-view.

I was asked to consult with the adjunctive therapist about this patient to explore how the milieu could become more supportive and beneficial to him. As I read his medical chart, social history and the results of his psychological testing it seemed to me that there was a consistent pattern in Richard's life of chaos. He'd been to many schools, despite only being in the third grade. He'd lived in many different homes and treatment facilities. I tried to imagine how the world must have looked to him. Words like chaotic, unsure, threatening and disappointing came to my mind.

I suggested to the adjunctive therapist that she talk to the psychiatric team about limiting Richard's activities and relationships. It was my sense that Richard desperately needed the stability that consistent and predictable relationships could offer him.

The team agreed to my suggestions and Richard was withdrawn from his activities and a small group of nurses and attendants was assembled to be his primary care givers. I was asked to provide individual art therapy sessions on a daily basis.

At first, Richard was literally all over the room. He opened drawers and cupboards, filled water containers, splashed in the sink, stuck his fingers in paint, knocked the trash can over, pulled paper towels from the dispenser and flicked the lights on and off, and . . . and . . . and. To watch him was to see a human derivation of the Tazmanian Devil cartoon character.

I began our therapy process by setting clear limits. Originally I scheduled fifteen-minute sessions. I insisted that he had to ask me before he touched things in the studio. When he did not comply with this simple rule I gave him one warning. If he continued to break the rule I would return him to the unit. There were several sessions which only lasted five or ten minutes. But gradually, as Richard became assured that no matter how badly he behaved on one day I would keep our appointment the next, he began to settle into a routine.

He would begin each session by growling, "I hate this darn place. What are we gonna do today?"

My response was always, "Richard, we're going to make something."

"What are we gonna make?" He'd respond.

"What would you like to make, Richard?"

This became our ritual of initiation. It was from these simple beginnings that Richard's creations grew. Several sessions into our therapy relationship Richard asked if he could make something out of cardboard. I told him that the only cardboard I had in the studio was from old boxes. He said, "that's just the kind I want."

When I brought two old boxes into the room he dove into them with his scissors. Without making any plan that I could see, he cut shapes, pasted and glued his rendition of the U. S. S. Enterprise. He worked for thirty minutes, non-stop.

The Enterprise was the first of a galaxy of cardboard creations. He made a Klingon warship, a Romulan vessel, Federation freighters, planets, suns and moons.

I have often wondered if his media of choice, cardboard, preferably of the discarded variety, in some way represented his sense of self, i.e., someone who had been thrown away by the adult world. I did not ask Richard about this. I saw no point in putting such an interpretation into words.

As Richard was able to work for longer periods of time in the art studio it was also noticed that he got into fewer arguments at school and on the living unit. It is my belief that his creation of a cardboard galaxy symbolically helped him to bring structure to the chaos of his own childhood universe. As he gave form to the chaotic discarded media he likewise brought structure to his own anarchy. Feelings, themes, conflicts and powerful forces were given form through the psychic salt of Richard's images.

11. Art as Hope

Without hope, it can be argued, there is no psychotherapy. I suspect that the same can be said of art, that where there is no hope, there can be no art. The art therapist must have hope for the patient and the patient must hope for herself. Making art is a symbolic expression of hope.

Judy and the Walls. Judy entered the studio quietly. 37 years old, but looking closer to 50 than 30. Her eyes were gray and dull. I knew, from having read the preliminary reports about her, that she had been a member of a gang since her late adolescence. She'd used pot daily, was an alcoholic and had occasionally snorted cocaine. She had a sunken, yet hard, appearance.

Judy had admitted herself to the hospital. She just showed up late one evening at the Emergency Services door where she told the clinician that she would either be admitted to the hospital that night or she'd be dead by the morning.

As she came into the studio her eyes were downcast, her hair unkempt, and her clothes smelled of stale cigarettes. As I gave her a tour of the building she stopped in front of a painting that hangs in the northeast corner. The image is an abstract portrait of an infant in utero. The mother stands with arched back as a swirl of dark colors surrounds her.

"Did you do that?" Judy asked.

"No. That painting was done by one of our adolescent patients last winter."

Judy looked at me suspiciously. "I suppose you wouldn't let him take it home!" There was an edge of defiant hostility to her voice.

"Oh no," I replied. "He could have taken it with him but he decided to leave it hanging here in the studio."

"Why would he do that?"

"Well, Judy, you'd really have to ask him to know for sure, but I think it was because he had a good experience at the hospital. He wanted to give something to the studio."

She grimaced. "That's a laugh. Who the hell has a good experience here?"

Overhearing this, Horace, a retired man who'd been in the art studio for about three weeks spoke, "I have."

Judy turned toward Horace. "Who asked you?" She sneered.

Horace looked at his sculpture uncomfortably. "Nobody asked. But I heard what you said to Bruce. Really lady, how do you expect him to answer your question? If he tells you that people sometimes end up liking it here, or that people get better here, you'll just say that he's feeding you a line of B. S. There's no way for him to win. I've been here a couple weeks and I've seen this same thing happen several times. New people come in feeling like death-warmed-over and Bruce tells them about how making art will help them. They look at him like he's nuts."

"Sounds loony tunes to me." Judy exclaimed.

Horace went back to his work, "You'll get out of this place what you put into it, lady."

Judy sarcastically yawned. "I'm so bored." She sighed.

I said, "You know Judy, boredom comes from an absence of quality relationships. I think Horace is right, you'll get what you give in the hospital. Let's get to work."

It is essential that we art therapists have a firm conviction that what we do is healthy and curative. If we have faith in the power of the creative process, if we trust it, our faith will be infectious. Art therapists must remain active artistically, for it is in the doing of art for ourselves that our faith is nurtured. It is in the studio that hope is kindled. Let's get to work.

12. Art as Benevolence

Making art is a transcendent activity. Often the patients I treat are ruthlessly self-indulgent. Their self-absorption takes the form of hopelessness, self critical introspection, and an inability to maintain authentic relationships. Since personal meaning can only be found in self-transcendence, it is a crucial aspect of the therapy process to engage the patient in situations which involve a thing outside the self. In the expressive group therapy context transcendent absorption is the norm. Patients respond to each other, and to each other's art. In this, an air of contagious benevolence is established.

Frances and Her Boxes. Frances had been in the expressive group for three sessions. She was a middle-aged editor of text books. A precise, rather controlling and cold woman, her drawings in the group were rigid and lifeless.

Bruce: (to the group) Today I want us to begin by drawing five circles on your page. Put your name at the top the page.

          Now, I'd like us to move around the room to other's pages and draw a symbol of your impressions of that person in one of their circles.

Frances: Oh, I don't think I could do that. I really don't know any of these people that well.

Peer: Lighten up, Frances. You know us as well as we know you.

Bruce: Give it your best effort, Frances. I'm sure that everybody is interested in how you see them.

Frances: I'll just do the same thing on everyone's page then. Will that make you happy? (glaring)

I did not respond to Frances's angry bait. The group members moved around the room attending to their images of one another.

A discussion period followed the drawing portion of the session. When it came time to discuss the images drawn on Frances's page the atmosphere of the group thickened. An air of tension filled the small group room.

Tony: Frances, I tried to draw a brick wall. You seem so hard on yourself to me. You never bend, 'least I ain't seen it.

Frances: Ain't is not proper grammar, Tony.

Patricia: Didn't you hear what Tony said, Frances?

Frances: I heard him quite distinctly.

Patricia: I drew the boxes. They are all the same color and the same size. They are all in order, but it looks to me like there's something missing, Frances.

Frances: Well, I . . .

Jim: I drew your circle as gray. I wish I knew more about Frances, but I just couldn't think of anything colorful to draw about you.

Frances: I . . . I . . . (tears welled up, she tried to fight them)

Bruce: It's alright, Frances. Let them come. Nobody here wants to hurt you, just let them come.

The dam burst, and years of tears poured from her. Patricia picked up the tissue box and placed it beside Frances's chair. She leaned over and gave her a hug.

In the art studio and the expressive group room patients meet their needs by giving to others. Sometimes the gifts are painful ones, sometimes gentle and supportive. They often encourage one another, sometimes criticize. They share artistic and life strategies. They make suggestions and listen to each other.

Benevolence. *Disposition to do good. An act of kindness. A generous gift.* [12]

The making of art is an inherently benevolent act for it is a gift to others, an offering to life itself.

Chapter XIV

PATHOS OR PATHOLOGY
(Sane or Sick)

In the early years of my professional life I often heard professionals from other disciplines express profound fears about the process of artistic expression. One psychiatrist was concerned that I encouraged, what he termed, "Sick imagery." It was his fear that to put disturbing emotional material into concrete imaginal forms was to support a lack of inner control. He and I argued on many occasions about whether expression or suppression was the treatment of choice for his patients. It has always been my position that expression is not harmful to people, but keeping secrets, bottling feelings up, most definitely is.

I believe that my psychiatrist colleague operated from a position that views artistic imagery (at least that produced by psychiatric patients) as pathological. Pathological, of course, means *altered or brought on by disease.* I, on the other hand, assert that creative endeavors are an expression of pathos—*an element in experience or in artistic representation evoking compassion.*

This polarity is a pivotal philosophic quandary for us art therapists. It represents the dominant approaches to imagery that pervade the art therapy profession. There are, I believe, four basic styles of relating to imagery.

The first style regards imaginal material as overt expressions of unconscious conflictual material. This model asserts that particular meanings can be ascribed to symbolic images. This approach has its roots in Freudian analysis.

In this model images are regarded as the servants of the *id* and are representations of powerful sexual and aggressive drives.

Art therapists who subscribe to this style of handling imagery often attempt to classify and catalogue images. These efforts inevitably lead to equations regarding the meaning of the image. For instance: snakes = phallic symbols; caves = vaginal openings; fires = rage. Such formulas invariably focus on a disease orientation, or dysfunctional aspect of the individual. From this perspective images are concrete representations of the *pathological.*

A second style of relating to imagery focuses on a pathological understanding of art products, and suggests that patients with certain types of psychiatric disorders create art that is similar enough as to allow classification. It follows then that art therapists who see the art work of a given individual may make a reasonable hypothesis regarding the appropriate diagnosis for the individual. For instance, if an art therapist from this school of thought believed that patients suffering from dysthymia use black and blue paint when given a choice, it would likely follow that when the art therapist saw a patient using black and blue paint she might presume that the patient was dysthymic.

It is clear that one is seldom diagnosed as being healthy and joyful. The process of diagnosis is reserved for those who already believe that something is wrong with them. In other words, to approach imagery from a diagnostician's perspective implies that images are manifestations of disease.

At the other philosophic pole from these *pathological* positions is the view of my Lesley College colleague, Shaun McNiff. In his workshops and writings Shaun offers the idea that "the image never comes to hurt you." In a 1991 lecture he shared the story of a dream image. The image was painted by a student during one of Shaun's workshops. It was of a dark Ninja who comes in the night, placing a black bag over the student's head. The student expressed much fear and anxiety regarding the Ninja.

Operating from his *pathos* perspective, Shaun suggested that perhaps the Ninja was presenting itself in the dream in an effort to help the woman dreamer get in touch with her feelings and to turn off her intellectualizations. From this perspective the image can be viewed as a benevolent force born of compassion.

In my work with students in the Clinical Internship in Art Therapy at Harding I have often encountered this same phenomenon. One former intern struggled repeatedly with the images of boxes that emerged in her drawings, both in groups with patients, and in peer group experiences. The box image initially represented the intern's style of compartmentalizing various aspects of her life. This walling-off served a defensive and inhibiting function in her life. Rather than view the boxes as symbols of repressed, conflictual material, or as indicators of dysfunction, we approached the boxes as important messages. By attending to them respectfully we came to know them as intriguing mysteries, inviting her to loosen her tight and constricting emotional controls. Over the course of her training the sharp edges and harsh dividing lines softened.

I believe that my images have a life of their own. They are my creations, of course, and in a sense are reflections of their creator. As evidence of this I suggest that you gather ten friends and ask them to tell you the story of one of your images, independently of one another. I guarantee that ten different stories will be recounted, and that they will be different from the story that you, the creator, would tell.

From such a perspective the image is a messenger or intermediary. It is not only an object of analytical inquiry, but a subject capable of teaching. If the image has a life of its own, with its own mission, then we who involve ourselves with it must regard our work as sacred. As art therapists we deal with living images and the living artists who made them. Both subjects command deep respect.

From this viewpoint it is impossible to establish any formula for interpretation or equation for analysis. To do so would be like performing an autopsy on the image. Autopsies are reserved for the dead. The reality is that *this* does not always mean *that.* In my work with the art of live patients $2 + 2$ often $= 13$. Images should not be seen as cadavers to be measured and pathologized. The world of the imagination is mist and shadows. As art therapists we must embrace the mystery and cultivate *devotional seeing.*[8] Our work often takes us into ambiguous worlds where nothing is absolute.

We art therapists have the option of handling the images of our patients, and our own, as infectious and diseased, or as living *ensouled* entities worthy of our most tender care and highest respect. The choice we make colors every aspect of our career. It affects how we relate to our patients/clients, our colleagues, and ourselves. I urge compassion over dissection, pathos over pathology.

Chapter XV

WHO, WHAT, WHERE, WHEN, WHY, HOW?

It is a tenet of the newspaper reporter's profession that good stories must include *who, what, where, when, why* and *how.*

In mystery novels it is always the task of the hero-detective to establish exactly what the crime was, where and when it was committed, how it was done, why it was perpetrated and ultimately who the culprit was.

For both reporters and detectives the process of interrogation is an integral component of the task at hand. Cross examination and penetrating query are essential skills for Clark Kent and Dick Tracy. This is not the case, however, with art therapists. We are not in the business of investigating a criminal, nor making public the unsavory details of a public figure's behavior.

The image of an archaeologist patiently dusting the ruins of some long past civilization is much the better analogy to our occupation. The archaeologist seeks not to disturb, but patiently and gently make visible.

As I work with the students who come to the Clinical Internship in Art Therapy, and my colleagues who participate in the Clinical Art Therapy Graduate Intensive Programs at Harding Hospital I tell them time and again, *dialogue with the image, don't interrogate it.* Cross examination and interrogation are tactics of intrusion and manipulation. As art therapists our effort must be toward encouraging the sharing of images in an atmosphere of mutual respect and honor.

Who, what, where, when, why and *how* questions set a tone of inquisition that is not conducive to sharing. These questions, as do those of the detective, seek the objective facts. When engaging with images, whether those of patient artists, colleagues, or my own, I find it most helpful to avoid the role of the inquisitor.

How is this done?

It is done through engagement with the story of the image. The story of the image may be one that the patient tells, or the one I hear as I look at the picture, or some combination of both possibilities.

167

Figure 15. I can almost hear the wind rustling . . .

An Example: Refer to Fig. 15:

In dealing with this painting an imaginal detective might begin with a question like this.

I. A.: "What is this building you have painted?"
Patient: "I'm not sure."
I. A.: "Who lives in this place? Who lives here?"
Patient: "I really don't know."
I. A.: "Do you have any idea where this building might be?"
Patient: "No."
I. A.: "When have you seen such a place?"
Patient: "I'm not sure."
I. A.: "Then why did you paint it?"
Patient: "I DON'T KNOW!"

When an art therapist operates from this interrogative mode little therapeutic work is done. Patients and clients tend to retreat into one word answers, in effect withdrawing from the art therapist. The search for the facts does little more than intimidate and alienate. I propose a different model of engagement with the images of my patients.

Bruce: "I look at your image and I can almost hear the wind rustling those curtains."
Patient: "I can feel it on my face."
Bruce: "Something about your painting reminds me of hot August afternoons."
Patient: "No, I was thinking of October. A cool, clear fall day.
Bruce: "Fall is a time of change."
Patient: "Uh huh."
Bruce: "I am drawn to the openings, the window and the door. They are inviting but mysterious too."
Patient: "Mysterious is a good word. It looks so dark in there, I think it's scarey."
Bruce: "I like the contrasts of the warm brown, stark white and cool blue."
Patient: "That's me alright."
Bruce: "I wonder. . . ."
Patient: "My friends say that I am hot and cold. I guess I can be moody."
Bruce: "You know, I feel a little lonely when I look at your image."
Patient: "Yes."
Bruce: "Sometimes people talk about houses and buildings as being symbols of themselves."

Patient: "I can sure relate to that."

In this brief interchange, rather than rely on who, what, where, when, why and how questions I used imaginal and sensual words. Wind rustling, hot, fall, mysterious, warm, stark, cool and wonder are words that invite imaginal thinking and interaction. By using language in this manner I enter a dialogue with the patient and the image, the point of which is not to categorize or label the image, (or the patient) but rather to be with and to understand. By invoking images through my use of these words, I honor the image-making process by responding to it on its own terms. The effort is not to unearth the *TRUTH* about the image or its maker; rather it is an effort to attend. By honoring the image I honor its maker.

As art therapists it is our most profound compliment to have the patient leave our presence with a solid sense of having been respected. The criminal villain seldom feels respected by the detective, nor does the subject of the investigative reporters queries.

Recently an Intern from our program came to supervision quite distraught. The art therapist who was supervising her in a satellite practicum had made an off-handed remark to the effect that the Harding style of doing art therapy is elitist. The satellite supervisor's position was that attending to the image in the way I described above is too time-consuming. She had told my student that things must be put into words directly and quickly and that engaging in imaginal dialogue was impractical.

My counsel to the Intern was this: if words are all that matter, the satellite supervisor is perhaps correct. However, there are many other disciplines whose main focus is cognitive discourse. I suggest that art therapists who long too strongly for things to be put into words are engaging in *elitist* mimicry of these other disciplines, i.e., psychiatry, psychology, social work and counseling.

It is the image that is the heart and soul of our professional identity. Our words must be used to honor and cherish images, not interrogate them. I encourage art therapists to avoid the *who, what, where, when, why how* mentality and embrace an attitude of awe and wonder.

Chapter XVI

THE THERAPEUTIC SELF

Since the beginning of civilization people have sought the wisdom of a special few. Dr. Sheldon Kopp refers to these as the "creative minority, to whom others turn for leadership, for guidance, for courage, for understanding, for beauty."[30]

As human beings we vary from one another. The members of one family exhibit profound differences. Even identical twins develop personality traits that set them apart from each other. Still there are some qualities of human existence that are common to us all: man, woman, oriental, occidental, African, primitive and modern. It can be argued that despite the diversity of our distinguishing characteristics, in the end our similarities outnumber our differences.

All of us, regardless of race, nationality, religion, socio-economic status, size or shape enter the world as powerless, needing the good will and care of those around us in order to survive. Each of us must find our niche in the family or situation upon which we depend. All of us travel the difficult path from infancy through childhood, adolescence, adulthood and old age.

As adults we struggle with the joys and sorrows of finding companions. We marry, raise children, achieve some sense of security and identity, only to have it fade in our later years. Ultimately, all of us must face death. The death of our loved ones, our friends and inevitably, ourselves is at the core of humankinds common experience of life.

Acknowledgment of the chaos and disquiet that accompanies these common experiences causes each society to create systems, belief structures, rituals and emissaries to support the journey of individual persons through the turbulence of life's passages. The profession of art therapy has developed metaverbal recognition of the way life is. In other times and other places this role was filled by shamans, witch doctors, clergy and and prophets. The art therapist is one of the current assignees to deal with the human struggle to survive and thrive.

From a theological standpoint the therapeutic relationship may be described in the traditional terms of the ministerial role: *Pastor, Priest* and *Prophet.* The tasks of the *pastor* are to care for, support, console and guide the members of his/her congregation. The *Priest* functions as the leader of the sacred rituals that, through symbolic action language, tell the essential story of the community. The *Prophet* reminds the community of the way their lives are. The Prophet's critical function is to focus attention on the reality that it is only through facing one's fears that meaning can be found.

As an art therapist I find myself continually comforting my patients, engaging them in the rituals of creation in the studio, and confronting their systems of denial about the way their lives are.

Art therapists engage in these tasks for the purpose of establishing a therapeutic relationship. At times our clients may see our work together as magical, drudgery, spiritual, supportive, challenging, comforting or afflicting. All of these attributes share the common root that the therapeutic relationship is established for the sake of good, for healthy change, for personal growth. Each manifestation of our work is aimed toward relief of suffering and each is effective when appropriately tied to the needs of the individual who has sought our service.

It is the therapist's responsibility to see beyond conventional thought and trends of the present. We must understand that what is hailed today as the latest wisdom offers only an illusory security.

As art therapists our historical connection to the role of the artist serves as the anchor for such creative courage. The artists of the world have always sought meanings that are deeper than the fads, laws and fashionable intellectual constructs of a given time. It is well documented that artists frequently view the formalities of their particular era as little more than entertainment for the masses.

The art therapist must understand the unspoken language of dream and myth. Myth and dream are the metaphoric images that contain and express deep truths about the individual's life, and the inner life of the surrounding culture.

By myth I mean the imaginal expression of humanity's most basic pleasures, struggles and uncertainties. I do not use *myth* in the parochial sense of being a frivolous fiction. On the contrary, myths are the insights of the world. They address the foundational human experiences which have been shared by all people in all times.

Dreams are to individuals what myths are to cultures. Dream images portray truths about the dreamer's inner life. Although they often have little to do with *fact,* they always present *truth* in symbolic form.

Art therapists bring to the therapeutic relationship a deep respect for the unspoken language of dream and myth. It is not our effort to translate, or interpret, these into rational constructs consistent with current thought. Rather, our effort is to kindle in our patients and clients a respect for that which is not logical, not sensible, yet still true about themselves and their world. In order to do this we must assure the client that images, whether dreamed or mythic, do not come to harm, they come to enlighten.

Therapists, regardless of disciplinary tradition, are often described as charismatic. "To have charisma is to possess the gift of grace."[30] At the core of art therapist's *charisma* is the awareness of freedom that comes as a result of artistic expression. Anything that can be painted can be reworked, or painted over. It is impossible to predict just what an artist will make next. The grace of our profession is nurtured through our capacity for innovation and our undaunting fearlessness in the face of creative challenge.

Our artistic traditions allow us to be ultimately concerned with what we are doing at any given moment. At the same time we must be content with doing only that which can be done. As the painter builds the stretcher frame she is not worried by what the final picture will, or will not, be. She must be satisfied with attending to construction. The charisma and grace of art therapists comes from our capacity to trust ourselves and the creative process. Making art has taught us not to worry about how we are doing. We expect to feel lost sometimes, to be afraid, to be uncertain and imperfect. When we embrace our fears and flaws we are no longer controlled by them. Every time we face an empty canvas we learn that nothing is certain, but if we trust ourselves and the process, the image will come. It is from these multiple experiences with media and work that we develop our capacity to console, lead, confront and struggle.

All therapists must wrestle with the difficult, recurring question of our level of transparency with our patients. What are our professional boundaries? What should we share about our lives with our patients? How closely should we guard our personal privacy? When and why do we share with our patients? These questions, and more, swirl together and gradually come into focus on the issues of openness between art therapist and patient.

As these questions are answered by experienced art therapist's there seems to be a continuum of responses ranging from opaqueness to transparency, with translucence approximately midway between.

OPAQUE	TRANSLUCENT	TRANSPARENT
All aspects of therapist's life are withheld from the patient.	The therapist is cautious regarding the sharing of personal information. The question is always asked, how will my sharing be helpful to the patient?	The therapy relationship is viewed as a mutual exchange of self revelations.

Each art therapist must decide for himself or herself where his/her therapeutic style falls on this continuum. When my students ask me for "the rules" regarding proper professional behavior in relation to self-disclosure, I tell them that they must experience the emptiness of a missed opportunity when they unnecessarily withheld information. Likewise, they must feel the pain of being abused by the patient who was not ready or able to respond positively to the gift of the therapist's vulnerability. These feelings must be experienced time and again in order for the trainee to develop a set of inner cues that encourage revelation or warn to withhold.

Regardless of which level of self disclosure one chooses, it is essential that self-awareness (disclosure of the self to the self) remain a top priority. In order to maintain our authenticity as art therapists we must be willing to constantly look in the creative mirror. We must allow ourselves to see ourselves honestly. Sometimes this is an easy process filled with excitement and joy. At other times it is terribly difficult, frightening and overwhelming. Sometimes the reflections in the mirror will be ugly, grotesque and disturbing. Sometimes we will see images of courage and compassion. It is our strength, as artists, therapists and art therapists to see our heroic and horrific, our foolish and funny, beautiful and beastly aspects. We can sometimes be opaque to our patients, but we can never be less than transparent to ourselves.

Finally, no discussion of therapeutic relationships can be complete without the inclusion of love. Confrontation, consolation, struggle, charisma and freedom are nothing if not in the context of love. "And if I have prophetic powers, and understand all mysteries and all knowledge, and if I have all faith, so as to remove mountains, but have not love, I am nothing."

It is not enough that an art therapist be a gifted technician. It is not enough to understand how to use the Diagnostic Service Manual, or developmental theories, or artistic techniques. The grace and charisma of the art therapist cannot be used only to extol her own power and uniqueness. The art therapist's gifts find meaning only when they are used in the context of benevolent offerings of possibility to another. To love is to maintain unselfish, loyal and altruistic concern for the good of another. The making of art is an act of love, as is the doing of therapy.

Chapter XVII

A PSYCHIATRIST'S VIEW
OF THE ARTS IN THERAPY

Dr. Robert Huestis is the Director of the Department of Psychiatry at Harding Hospital. He is a past medical director of the Adolescent Integrated Program, and is currently the director of the Admissions and Crisis Service at Harding.

Introduction

The role of the art therapist in the mental health treatment team is defined at least as much by the team leader, usually a psychiatrist, as it is by the art therapist. If the team leader has little appreciation, tolerance or understanding of the value of art therapy, that attitude will be mirrored by the other team members immediately. The leader's power to do this is why great care should go into the selection of a team leader.

Having established the necessity of team acceptance, it can be said that the role of the art therapist in the psychiatric team is defined by the interplay between the *leadership ability* of the leader and the team *abilities* of the art therapist.

The ideal treatment team has a diversity of talents, strengths, weaknesses and points of view. The ideal team leader is one who has at least these four qualities or characteristics:

One, the ability to set a tone of active inquiry, founded upon a respect for the uniqueness and complexity of each patient;

Two, a respect for the professions as well as the talents of individual team members, conveying to them their importance in developing and carrying out the overall treatment plan;

Three, an ability to weave the threads of diverse information into a dynamic pattern that will reveal the individual patient's situation at a given time. This is critical, for it is from such dynamic understanding that therapeutic interventions are prescribed.

Four, a commitment to assure the active team participation of those therapists who deal primarily in non-verbal modalities. In the often hectic, hyperkinetic, verbal environment of the team meetings, non-verbal therapies like art therapy can be overlooked.

It is important to understand these challenges to becoming an active and effective team member. If the psychiatrist team leader is less than ideal (a certainty), it is also a certainty that the art therapist will have to adapt. My observation is that the effective team art therapist adapts along the lines of *thoughtful assertion* that has its own developmental phases. This development seems to be as predictable as physical development milestones in infants or the milestones in artistic evolution—random scribbling through early schema to naturalism and abstraction.

Development of the Team Art Therapist

In over fifteen years of observing and leading psychiatric treatment teams, I have noted that there is an evolutionary process that produces *thoughtful assertion.* The role that art therapists play on the team depends upon their evolutionary position. This is true for both experienced art therapists and novices. To illustrate: imagine an "evolutionary tree." The trunk of this tree is a sense of professional security. That is the belief, fostered from both inside and outside experiences of the therapist, that the arts provide a unique piece of the therapeutic puzzle. The roots of the tree are the art processes themselves and the entire history of art. The art therapist who comes to team meetings with a secure sense of what art therapy is all about and how he or she relates to it, has an enormous leg-up on being an effective member of the team. On the other hand, those who are caught in personal or professional identity crises and do not see themselves as truly equal with other disciplines, tend to be timid members who don't venture forth with observations and interpretations when they are most needed, i.e., when the clinical picture is difficult to understand and the treatment process is stuck. A sense of personal security is especially important in art therapy, since its interventions are done non-verbally, while the rest of the mental health professions are so enamored of the spoken word. A secure person is much more likely to venture forth with a needed contribution.

A significant evolutionary branch is the ability to hold on to one's unique identity within a team structure. I have observed that the art therapist has a particularly difficult time with this, because the nature of mental health teams is so verbal and analytical while the art therapist's identity rests in the metaverbal or non-verbal Gestalt.

The security to let art stand on its own seems to me to be a struggle throughout the art world. At a recent exhibit of George Bellows's work, I stood observing "Stag at Sharkey's." I was aware of my inner experience of power, drama and struggle. The image stayed with me until I came to the end of the exhibit. There I was greeted with an overlay of the painting, with multiple lines "educating" me as to how the artist used a series of geometric triangles to create the picture. What a letdown! How quickly the former image and my former inner emotional experience faded!

Similarly, in teams I have seen powerful images and insights evaporate with excessive verbal analysis. The art therapist who is secure enough in his or her own identity to bring, share and educate members of the team with actual artistic productions of the patient, is a powerful advocate for the patient and for the discipline. In short, use non-verbal pathways to emphasize the metaverbal nature of the art therapy experience.

At the same time that one is working on securing one's professional identity, the art therapist must strive to become a team player. If one expects the art therapy discipline to be respected, the art therapist must have respect for other professional disciplines and their interventions. It is important for the art therapist, who has a special power with patients who have some artistic interest, to reinforce the value of the other parts of the treatment plan that don't have an "artsy" flavor. For instance: one patient on our adolescent unit was a fairly skilled artist, but he was so angry at his family that he refused to meet with them and the social worker for scheduled sessions. This went on for several weeks. The art therapist working with the patient served as a gentle persuader, subtly supporting the need to work things out with his parents, in the same way the patient was able to work through difficult design problems in his painting. The art therapist pointed out that the patient did not let his anger keep him away from the studio, nor should it keep him out of the family therapy session.

As the leader of the treatment team, how do I know I have team players? One of the surest ways is to ask the *patient* about how confidentiality works on his team. If the patient understands that he is covered by team confidentiality, I know he is surrounded by team players. Team confidentiality means that the patient understands that what he produces in any therapeutic activity will be shared with all team members, but will not go outside the team. There is always the temptation to view one's work as just a little more important than someone else's. Professional pride is good, but when it leads to "special deals" between patient and staff, it is destructive. All special deals backfire because they involve holding back clinical/milieu material. Holding back information quickly labels one as a non-team player. Because of the highly individualistic nature of artistic production, I have seen beginning art therapists struggle with sharing therapeutic information with other team members. It is a constant struggle with patients to make it clear that, while artistic production is individualistic, keeping part or all of the artistic experience outside team is a blueprint for therapeutic trouble and team alienation.

This idea of sharing information also applies to information that might be "different" from what other team members are reporting—that your interaction with the patient is not the same as theirs. It may be positive, e.g., that in Expressive Art he isn't obnoxious, hard to engage or unwilling to share. Often times there is the tendency to withhold negative material, out of fear that it will personally reflect on you or your ability as a therapist. Once your professional identity is secure, it will be easier to see that to a well-functioning team, it is just as important to know who isn't working in an activity, who is making personal attacks on the therapist, or who is devaluing any part of their treatment program. The therapist who reports only successes and triumphs and no personal discomfort is suspect as a team player.

The mental set that is most helpful in team meetings is a respect for different views of the same patient. Differences are interesting. There would be no need to have team meetings if everyone was going to say the same thing. The best therapists and team leaders can tolerate some ambiguity and wait for the picture to unfold, much like an artist must tolerate not knowing how a painting will end up.

Another important branch in the development of thoughtful assertion is knowing what kinds of individuals will benefit most from art therapy activities as well as when to initiate them. As one builds an identity, these kinds of decisions should become easier, as long as the art therapist is guarding against his own complacency: engaging only those individuals that make him feel comfortable and avoiding those patients that challenge him or stimulate unpleasant affect.

This is a complicated matter, for on the one hand it might be argued that the process of making art is intrinsically therapeutic for all persons. However, in the setting of the psychiatric institution, often operating under constraints of time and resources, it is essential that therapeutic interventions be made in a way that is efficient, both psychologically and fiscally.

The art therapist must develop a sense of who he works most efficiently with. At the same time he must not be so narrow in self-evaluation of efficacy as to exclude groupings of patients with whom he has had little or no experience.

It is perfectly natural that, early in their careers, art therapists will be drawn to patients who share their interest in art. In a sense, such patients mirror the values of the novice therapist, making interaction both pleasant and meaningful. As the art therapist matures, less of this mirroring quality is required. The professional challenge to the developing art therapist is to gradually expand the variety of patients he or she can work with effectively. Eventually, one's professional competence includes patients who may openly state that they detest art.

Two key aspects of this evolutionary process are honesty and confidence. You must be honest enough in a team setting to speak up when you feel you cannot handle working with a given patient. There is nothing wrong in knowing and sharing your limitations. On the contrary, damage can be done if you allow yourself to overextend your competency.

Likewise, you must develop confidence in your own strengths. It is inappropriate to accept only those patients who reflect your interests and values.

It is crucial that art therapy students and novice practitioners not expect themselves to be experts on the first day of their professional life.

Team Process

To the beginning art therapist, a psychiatric team meeting may seem chaotic, unfocused and superficial. Questions arise. *How can a team effectively deal with the treatment plans of seven or eight patients in an hour? What's my role? When do I speak up?*

These are normal, perhaps even essential questions for the novice art therapist to wrestle with. Teams can be understood only if there is an organizing schema that is specific enough to be directive but broad enough to include all data. Any delineation carries with it the drawbacks of reductionism. A picture of all the parts of a carbureter tells you much less than a picture of it as part of a motor. The schema that I have found helpful in my own evolutionary process is to think of a treatment encounter as being divided into three distinct but overlapping phases. The word *overlapping* is probably the most important word in that last sentence because very few, if any, psychiatric patients get better in a linear fashion.

The three phases of treatment can be labeled in a variety of ways. I have chosen one developed by Donald Rinsley, M.D. It consists of 1) resistance; 2) working through; 3) termination. It cannot be over-emphasized that patients in their encounters with *different* aspects of the treatment milieu can present *different* phases in *different* activities or with *different* therapists. It is the norm, for example, for an adolescent to be resistive in parts of the treatment milieu while at the same time be in the working through or even termination phase with others. In the psychiatric treatment milieu it is not uncommon to have a patient reacting and behaving angrily on the unit (in the living environment). These patients may be verbally abusive to nursing staff, resist participation in unit activities and struggle with rules and authority. Yet these same patients may be positively involved in the art studio, rather neutral in school, while working very hard in individual therapy.

A parallel process to these three phases can be observed in the realm of the artist. As a painter faces the blank canvas she often experiences feelings similar to those associated with the resistance phase of treatment. The task seems overwhelming, filled with possibilities and problems. Many artists speak of the hardest brush strokes being the first, just as many patients report that the hardest part of therapy is beginning.

As the image emerges, the artist is filled with the excitement and energy of the working through phase. This is a period of introspection, reflection and meaningful work.

As the painting nears completion, the artist has conflictual experiences of joy and loss. The termination is marked by the event of signing the painting, but this moment only symbolizes the complex process of summing up, bringing to a close, mourning and letting go.

This process is rarely linear in the artist. Some days, even after a good start, the canvas can again appear blank. Or just when it is time to sign the painting, a new vision may occur and major parts of the canvas are reworked.

In dealing with the resistance phase, the most important aspect is recognizing that the patient is in resistance and that resistance can be disguised with a pleasant and seductive veneer. Resistance is defined as the presentation of oneself by denying 1) the existence of disturbing behavioral patterns; 2) their consequences; or 3) the inner experience surrounding that behavior.

The second important aspect is to pick up the primary patterns of resistance, thus enabling the therapist to pick the right intervention. The third part to remember about the resistance phase is that the effective team leader will be most interested in the art therapist's comments on the quality *not* of the artistic productions, but the quality of the relationship between the patient and therapist. The questions in team follow this theme: *Are you hooking the patient into a workable therapeutic alliance? How does the patient respond to a group setting? Does he have artistic strengths? Can he accept praise and/or criticism from staff/peers?* Once it is clear that the relationship is present, it is time for the team to turn its attention to the canvas.

The second phase, working through, is usually heralded by the patient taking some ownership for her present difficulty and is almost always associated with some degree of becoming connected to her own inner experience. It does not necessarily mean an ability to put any of this into words. In general, through the skillful application of varied therapeutic modalities, the individual in this phase gradually exchanges old distorted views of herself (introjects) for new and less defeating ones. During this phase, I become intensely interested in the image content of the patient's productions. If we have identified separation/individuation as a primary conflict, is it there on the canvas? Do the artistic productions reflect a further integration of the conflict? Do the artistic productions show conflicts not yet appreciated? Do the themes seen in art therapy confirm and reinforce what we are learning from other professions and disciplines?

The termination phase is a period of consolidation and internalization of the gains made during the treatment process. It is a readying to leave the treatment process, but most important, readying oneself to separate from those individuals who have been most important during the patient's stay. This is a time when she learns that the helpful relationships are those that she can take with her in the form of both conscious and unconscious memories of the experiences shared with significant treaters. Ideally, the patient has developed a measure of confidence that she can recreate these relationships in some part after leaving the hospital. During this phase I look to the arts to provide the patient with a mechanism to express her sense of loss as she ends relationships. The feelings are often too difficult to put into words, but are profoundly expressed in images. In addition, artistic productions serve as ideal transitional objects: something given or received that is a tangible external representation of the inner experience.

Art as Part of the Unit or Milieu

There is one indirect way that the art therapist can educate the team and enhance the treatment milieu. Besides bringing patient art to the team meetings, she can encourage the authorized use of patient art in the decor of the inpatient living areas. Our unit has certainly been enriched as we have replaced the art selected by an interior designer with our patients' art. It has had the effect of giving a potent non-verbal message that *this is a place where patients count and serious work is attempted and appreciated.* There has been a related phenomenon of patients giving pieces of art work to the unit upon the occasion of their discharge. This has become fairly common and has pushed us to do some thinking about the meaning of the gifts. We have identified four distinct motivations:

1. **Affirmation.** Departing patients often long to demonstrate to the unit staff their positive feelings about the therapy experience. The leaving behind of a "goodbye painting" is an affirmation of the patient's positive regard for the staff and the treatment process.

2. **The Closet Effect.** As older adolescent and young adults move out of their parents' home, whether to college or to an apartment of their own, they often leave behind personal belongings in the closets. Whether conscious or not, this has the effect of leaving a part of themselves in the safety of parental care.

The closet effect of the departing patient serves the same purpose, i.e., symbolically maintaining a connection to the safe, nurturing and predictable treatment milieu. This serves to soothe some of the anxiety stimulated by separation.

3. **Giving Back.** Often the terminating patient longs to give back a part of himself to the treatment team. In a sense this honors the giving that the staff have done during the hospitalization.

4. **Concretization of Introject Exchange.** Most subtle is the idea that leaving an object of art behind represents a concretization of the exchange of introjects which has occurred within the patient during the treatment process. When the patient is first admitted, it is assumed that his self-view is negative. He has had countless interchanges over time that have solidified a negative self-concept. A major purpose of hospital treatment is to provide the patient many experiences with both neutral and positive emotional undertones. This is done through encounters with the

treatment personnel. Gradually the patient begins to reshape his sense of self as he experiences healthy interchanges with the staff. In short, an exchange of introjects occurs. The leaving behind of the art work becomes a concrete symbol of this process. The metaphoric message from the patient is, *You knew me when I was bad, yet you stuck with me. Now that I feel better about myself, I want to leave this symbolic object behind as testimony to the work we did.*

Summary

As part of the team building process, I try to meet with every new team member the first week he or she joins us. This is what I try to cover during that meeting:

Being part of a treatment team can be a challenging, exciting and anxiety-producing experience. Expect a little confusion as you search for and find your niche. Speak up in team; no one else will speak as well as you about the information that you have. Don't burden yourself with the expectation that you will be the "old hand" after one week. Trust the group process and support system that a team can provide. Art therapy doesn't need to be sold any more than psychotherapy or psychopharmacology. It will be effective with some patients, but not all. You will learn far more by appreciating differences than similarities. Finally, relax and have some fun.

Chapter XVIII

THINGS TO WORRY ABOUT

It Costs Too Much To Care

As I near the completion of the writing of this book in the mid-summer of 1993 it is a difficult time in the health care professions. Art Therapy is not immune to the economic pressures that are strangling mental health services everywhere in the world. In the past year some fine art therapy education programs have closed their doors because of insufficient funding from universities and state governments. At the same time there have been radical changes in the insurance industry which have resulted in profound changes in health care service delivery systems. This has caused significant "downsizing" and closing of private and state hospitals. Physical and mental health in the United States has become a political hot potato that accounts for much of the annual increase in the federal deficit. A spiraling system of increasing technology spurs ever rising costs that shrink the availability of care. The well-being of individual patients has been reduced to concrete measures in dollars and cents. Treatment of chronic illness, whether psychic or somatic, has been labeled a bad investment and resources have been allocated elsewhere. The pressures for reimbursement have led to exorbitant physician's fees, unconscionable use of medication and charges for procedures, with catastrophic effect on the sick person.

Dr. Bertram Brown, former Director of the National Institute of Mental Health (N. I. M. H.) once predicted that the creative arts therapies would become a most significant social movement of the 1990's. The time is now. Despite the economic trauma that has afflicted the health care industry, art therapy continues to grow in demand and popularity. It is becoming common for art therapists to work independently of the established, and ailing, health care institutions. More and more art therapists are establishing private practice offices, competing successfully with older helping professions: psychiatry, psychology and social work. This is happening partly out of necessity, and partly in response to demand from the consumer.

Commensurate with the increases noted above, there have been parallel movements in art therapy fee structures. As art therapists are approved for third party payment, there is a temptation to inflate professional fees. This is a matter of great concern, for it shadows the rise in physician costs that have so crippled the helping industry. As art therapists we have a moral imperative not to charge what the market will bear. Rather, we must strike an ethical balance between the capacity of our clients to pay, our need to make a profit and our ultimate concern for the lives of our patients. We must avoid the greed that seems to have overtaken much of the health care industry. The only way to do this is to stay intimately tied to our collective artistic heritage. I do not intend to imply that art therapists should take a vow of poverty. However, I do want to state that we have an opportunity to handle the financial aspects of our professional lives in a more responsible manner than many of our professional colleagues of other disciplines. Artists have always understood that their primary motivation is not monetary gain but rather the expression itself. Artist-therapists do well to keep this aspect of our professional roots in mind as we set fee structures for private and third party payors alike.

Perils of Promotion

As the art therapy profession has moved toward being a Masters Degree level of entry discipline many art therapists, relatively early in their careers, find themselves surrounded in the work place by Bachelors level colleagues. Music therapy, horticulture therapy, recreation therapy, occupational therapy and other action-oriented therapies have not moved to masters level educational requirements. Thus art therapists are often prematurely promoted to positions of clinical supervisor and program director by virtue of their advanced educational experience.

On the surface promotion is always an attractive event in the life of the young therapist. Promotion brings with it more money, prestige, political and programmatic power within the treatment system. Any time one is offered more money, more freedom, and more control the temptation is strong to accept without question.

There is, however, a darker side to this. Promotion usually means increased pressure, increased responsibilities for documentation, and increased administrative demands. At the same time there is a parallel decrease in patient contact, studio art time, and gradual isolation from those who once were peers but are now supervisees or employees.

The factors that motivated the art therapy novice to seek the profession, i.e., a belief in the essential goodness of art making processes, a desire to use the arts as a means of helping humanity, and a genuine longing to make a difference in the world, are all too easily subverted by the lure of earning power, ego inflation and control issues.

While it is certainly not impossible for an art therapist to become a clinical supervisor or program director and remain true to his original intentions, it is very easy for these to get lost in the shuffle. The heart and soul of the art therapy profession is found in the contexts of the art studio and the therapeutic relationship. It has been my experience that these qualities are often absent from the offices and job descriptions of program directors and clinical supervisors. It is not that these are bad people who intentionally pulled away from their professional foundation. It is that the pressures of administration and supervision are subtle, covert and deadening to the creative spirit. I have known art therapists who have lost their way so gradually that it is impossible to pinpoint any one time period or event that represents the beginning of their lostness. It is, like trying to mark the exact spot where fog begins or ends, nearly impossible and probably irrelevant. Irrelevant because knowing the facts of when and why do little to alleviate the suffering attached to such crises. I have had occasion to offer solace to such colleagues when they have sought my advice. My suggestion to them is always the same, "Go into your studio and paint about this." My intent in offering these words is to encourage my colleagues to go to their source, to listen to their own creativity, and to seek their own solutions to the dilemmas they face.

I worry about this not only from the abstract position of the detached observer. I have wrestled with these issues in my own career. There was a period of time in my professional life when I was off track. Seduced by title and authority I cut myself off from the very phenomena which captured my heart and imagination two decades ago. It was serendipitous that an arts experience profoundly reminded me of how and why I became an art therapist in the first place. I came into the field not expecting to become wealthy, not longing to be the boss, not wanting to spend my days behind a desk filling out evaluation forms, disinterested in the business of mental health care. I came to the profession out of love, creative energy and the internal drive to connect with my fellow human beings through art. I was fortunate that I was in a position to extricate myself from the energy draining and creativity sapping aspects of my work. I was able to give up my wish for control and advancement in exchange for my professional integrity. I have much less institutional political clout in 1993 than I did in 1988 and I have less command of my time and duties. In place of *cloutcom* I now have patient contact and studio time. I have gone back to my source. But I worry about these things.

It's Just a Picture

Not long ago a patient with whom I had worked in art therapy for a few weeks came by the studio to say good-bye. He shook my hand, said thank you, and was about to leave when I remembered that he had a painting in the drying rack. "Don't forget to take your painting." I said.

He turned back to look at me, "Oh I think I'll leave it here."

I was surprised. He had worked diligently on the piece and the end product was both pleasing and expressive. "Why would you leave it here?"

"Ah I don't know. I don't have any place to put it at home and I'm afraid it will remind me of how I felt when I came in to the hospital. Besides, it's just a picture." With that he turned and left the building.

Later that afternoon as I cleaned up after a session of adolescent studio art I ran across his painting. I pulled it from the rack and was caught by a wave of sadness. It's just a picture, he'd said. Just a picture.

As I sat looking at the painting a student entered the room. "Isn't that Tom's painting?"

"Yes." I replied.

"I thought he was getting discharged today?"

"He was. He stopped in to say good-bye this morning."

"But he didn't take his painting."

"No, he said it might bring back bad memories."

"Oh well," she said. "I guess we can gesso over it tomorrow."

"No. I think I'll hold onto it for awhile."

These brief interchanges highlight several significant ethical dilemmas that art therapists must grapple with which other therapy disciplines are exempt from. These are not covered in the Code of Ethics of the American Art Therapy Association,[31] for they have to do with how we attend to the images of our patients and thus cannot be codified.

- How do we regard images?
- How should we deal with art products abandoned by our patients?
- What should our response be to patient/artists who inform us that they intend to leave their work behind?

- Who owns the left-behind-art?
- Is gesso-ing over a piece an act of imagicide?
- Is it really just a picture?

If one views the image and the product as being merely inanimate objects made in the service of a therapeutic process then it is relatively easy to dismiss the questions above as irrelevant. If, however, one regards images and works as having a life of their own, separate and distinct from the maker, such questions become the center of ethical considerations.

I wanted to shout to Tom, "No, you can't leave these here. They came through you. They came to share with you. How dare you leave them behind!" But I didn't shout. I didn't even mildly protest. And so I am left *in loco parentis* of Tom's images. I cannot throw them away. I will not gesso over them. I have no right to display them. I hold their tender and turbulent messages in my heart and I worry about what to do.

Security, Sanctity and Severance

There is a brief line of dialogue in the 16mm film, *Why Man Creates*, [32] which expresses the notion that all radical ideas eventually become institutions which in turn reject radical new ideas. A quarter of a century ago art therapy was a radical new idea. In the twenty-five ensuing years the profession, though still quite young, has done much to institutionalize itself. Rigorous standards of art therapy education have been established. Strict and arduous credentialing systems have been devised. The American Art Therapy Association has been authorized to govern and nurture the development of the profession on a national scale. A demanding process of training site approval has been formed and ethical standards of patient care have been agreed upon by the majority of practicing art therapists. Corporations have been founded, by-laws written, certification examinations are on their way and consequences for non-compliance with the above have been delineated. There are schools of art therapy both at the undergraduate and graduate levels. Art Therapy has become an institution.

A disturbing aspect of the formalizing of the discipline is a growing trend toward forced uniformity of theory, philosophy and approach. As our specialty becomes more clearly defined there is tremendous temptation to insist on a narrow set of common understandings. This is a disturbing trend for it severs our connection with our own history, our roots.

The pioneers who forged the earliest identity of the art therapist came from a variety of educational, philosophical and experiential backgrounds. Some came from psychological and psychoanalysis. Some from psychiatry and the medical model. Others found their way into the infant field by way of professional art while still others came via ministry. It is glaringly evident that several of art therapy's founding mothers and fathers would not be allowed entry into the profession under today's standards.

The *radical new idea* of art therapy has been institutionalized in an effort to establish professional respectability and security. While there is obviously nothing inherently wrong with respectability and security, the side effects have a malignant tone. Theoriticians who have strayed outside the mainstream of thought have found themselves to be the target of criticism from without and within the profession. A cursory examination of published reviews of art therapy literature confirms that we are not always kind to one another. When we gather together is, almost always, an undertone of covert philosophic warfare that borders on corporate sucidality.

I wish to go on record here that while I passionately believe every word that I have written in this book, I hold no illusions that my way is the only way to do art therapy. It is just my way. I am not RIGHT. The ideas presented in this book are representative of one way to do the work. It is, I think, a good way, but it is only one of many good ways. Just as the abstract expressionists are no less artists than the surrealists, or the primitives or the minimalists, or the impressionists, or the . . . or the . . . etc. So, too, the analytic thinkers are no less art therapists than the gestalt art therapists, or the existential art therapists, or the behavioral art therapists, or the eclectic art therapists, or . . . or . . . or. If you want to drive from the east coast to the west coast there are many different roads that you take there.

The sanctity of the art therapy profession ultimately is tied to our capacity to embrace difference. The first word of our disciplinary name, ART, denotes a willingness to incorporate contrast and diversity into the "big picture." This is what artists have done from the beginning of time. As was noted earlier in this text, F. Scott Fitzgerald once commented that, the measure of a fine mind is the capacity to hold two opposing ideas as true. Surely it is the sacred task of the individual art therapist, and the institutions of art therapy alike, to hold in tension the possibility of multiple polar truths about this profession.

The institutions of art therapy must, in the near future, reevaluate their by-laws, standards and unspoken mores. The windows and doors of the building must be opened, for the air is getting stale within. I worry about our suffocating one another.

Chapter XIX

NOWHERE TO HIDE

If Nietzsche was correct, that only artists dare to show us the human being as he is, then it is a primary task of art therapists to engage with people without the aid of disguises or make-up. We must allow ourselves to be who we are without guile or manipulative intent. We must make our art in the company of patients as we encourage them to make theirs as we attend. As we look for the unique and authentic self of our patient that has often been scarred or hidden deep within, we cannot help but encounter our own disfigurements and concealed facets. I have often wondered if this fact rests at the root of why so many art therapists cease to function as artists outside the confines of the work environment. So much energy is spent in the therapeutic context that it may seem a daunting task to explore one's own caverns continually.

As a people we Westerners have become comfortable with the portraits of self created in the darkrooms of the studio photographer. Pleasant backdrops, filtered lenses, warm light and retouching techniques provide us with pictures of the selves we wish we were. No pimples, no scars, no unnecessary wrinkles. These are unauthentic portraits that have become the norm. But artists dare to paint reality, whether representational or abstract, they show us ourselves as we really are.

I believe that the task of all art is to depict what is real and genuine about life. All art has an existential quality. When I had just finished my first book, *Existential Art Therapy: The Canvas Mirror,* Shaun McNiff told me during a telephone conversation that the title was redundant. He said, "Everything about art is existential, and everything about existentialism is art." The aim of art, and art therapy, is to get beneath the surface of things. Once there, to use the gentle touch of the archaeologist, to brush away the emotional debris of life and make room for more life. It is the task of the scientist to theorize and prove the way things are. It is the task of the artist to express the way things feel. The facts are irrelevant if the images and the feelings associated with them are true. Artists give the world pictures of what it means to be alive in a certain time and place. The anguish, vitality and turbulent intensity of existence is the essential subject of inquiry for art therapy.

I have said elsewhere that, as a practicing artist, my work has comforted me in times of great stress and afflicted me in times of comfort. Sometimes I look at my paintings (children) and I am caught off guard by the courage and integrity I see. At other moments I am sickened by the oozing, pussing open wounds, haunted by the loneliness and embarrassed by the cowardice I see. The dilemma I face as an artist, and an existential art therapist, is that I cannot run from the anguish these images bring me. Not that I haven't tried, ... it doesn't work. The faster I run the quicker I am overtaken by the reality of my creation. There is no escape.

I know that as I form these words on the screen of my computer monitor they inevitably fail to convey the depth of my passion for this profession. In the process of writing, or reading, a book one is left ultimately in the shallow regions. Art and art therapy are not subjects of academic investigation alone. You must *make* art. You must *do* art therapy in order to really understand this *Introduction to Art Therapy.* The most I can hope for is that the stories and ideas I have shared here will pique your interest. If I can do this skillfully and with integrity, perhaps you will be drawn into the profession as I was twenty years ago.

I feel a deep sense of gratitude to the art therapists of a generation ago. Those who pioneered the field, breathed life into the national association and struggled to define a new and radical (yet old and proven) idea, that making art is a healthy thing to do. Without the likes of Don Jones, Felice Cohen, Bob Ault, Myra Levick, Bernie Stone, Eleanor Uhlman, Margaret Naumberg, Joe Garai, Janie Rhyne, Ben Ploder, Mary Huntoon, Bernie Levy and many others it is probable that my life would have taken a very different direction. I also feel a profound sense of responsibility to the art therapists yet to come. In every circumstance of my professional life I am cognizant of the fact that I am forced to choose my roads carefully, not only for my own well being, but for the sake of the well being of others. As an existential art therapist I am constantly in the company of the art works of my patients, colleagues and students. The entire focus of these encounters is the mutual growth that is made possible through shared imaginal experiences.

As an art therapy educator I am keenly attentive to the images that emerge as my students progress in the Clinical Internship in Art Therapy at Harding Hospital. The concentration here is on the deepening and broadening of the student's understanding of herself as an artist/

therapist. The Interns' images invariably depict their process of coming to grips with the angst they experience as they move from novice to graduate. I try always to be present and open to them as we meet together to reflect on their experience of themselves as artist-therapists.

As I work on my paintings I feel responsible to the art and to myself. Daily I paint in the company of my patients and colleagues, still the making of art is ultimately a solitary activity. As I stand before the blank canvas I am intensely aware of my aloneness. The tightly stretched canvas surface is not only an objective thing to be addressed, but an inner reality as well. It calls to me to free it from its empty blankness. As my brush moves across the tension of the canvas something deep within me vibrates and trembles as well. I believe that it is imperative that art therapists remain active artistically if they are to have any connection to the soul of their profession. If you are not committed equally to making art and serving humanity, choose another path for your life.

I regard the work that I do as sacred. Every time a patient dips their woundedness in acrylic paint, or dusts it with chalk, he receives the nourishment and courage that his life's journey demands. The therapy is not found in helping the patient rise above suffering, rather it is found in knowing how and when to immerse oneself in the creative flow.

My belief in the power and goodness of the art making process is contagious. I don't have to tell my patients or my students that I have faith in this. It oozes from my skin and is exhaled in the air I breathe. They see my faith with their own eyes. I don't have to talk about my concern that art therapists should remain active artistically. They will smell my sweat and see my commitment. Students, patients, and colleagues alike do not have to fear that I will leave them stranded in the midst of their journey. I will stand with them, and welcome them in the studio. We will make art.

"Walk with me," I tell them. "Let us baptize our wounds in paint and draw the strength and courage we need to continue our journeys. We have nothing and nowhere to hide."

Figure 16. Walk with me.

EPILOGUE

It is no doubt presumptuous to expect that this book has completely introduced the complex and diverse field of art therapy as it is now practiced in the United States. Still, perhaps to presume is an act of imagination. If that is so then I must pretend that I have adequately presented a text which touches the major themes and issues of the profession.

It is my deepest hope that this might be the first book, or one of them, that students new to the field read about art therapy. I am willing to imagine that the strengths of this text are in its constant reference to art making processes, and human compassion. It is my desire that readers will finish this book with a good feeling about the discipline. I fantasize them laying the book aside and saying, "Art therapy is a humane field which is ultimately concerned with love and images." If this apotheosis is true at all then I have been successful in creating the introduction I set out to make.

To be sure there are shortcomings to this book. I do not acquaint the reader with theories of symbolic equations, nor do I provide information regarding the scientific use of art as therapy. I cannot (will not) write about what I do not believe. Yet, this is no doubt a deficiency in my work. So be it. There are also patient populations that I have not attempted to address. I have not, for example, referred to the use of art therapy with the mentally retarded, or persons with AIDS, or the hearing impaired. I have provided clinical service to each of these specific populations but the basic tenets of the field I find applicable to all human beings. I will leave the writing of art therapy books for particular diagnostic categories to others in the profession. The core of the work is the same.

Our journey through this book is nearly complete. We have travelled a highway adorned with images, blood, metaphor, passion and mystery. I hope you have enjoyed the ride and I pray that you have felt the deep joy and passion that I have for the work. I feel truly blessed to have come upon the profession of art therapy. Each Monday morning I look forward to getting out of bed and going to work. I love what I do and I would likely do it as a volunteer was I not fortunate enough to be paid for my labor.

I have attempted to present the essence of the field as faithfully as I can. Our roots lay in two continents, the land of art, and the land of psychotherapy. We must always straddle these gracefully, with care and balance. We must always make art, and we must love. This is art therapy.

Peace,

B. L. M.

BIBLIOGRAPHY

1. McLean, Don. (1971) *An american pie.* (LP) New York: United Artists Records.
2. Whyte, D. (1990) *Where many rivers meet.* Langley, WA: Many Rivers Press.
3. Moon, B. (1990) *Existential art therapy: the canvas mirror.* Springfield, IL: Charles C Thomas.
4. Frankl, V. (1969) *Man's search for meaning: an introduction to logotherapy.* Philadelphia: Washington Square Press.
5. Fromm, E. (1956) *The art of loving.* New York: Harper & Row.
6. McNiff, S. (1983) *The arts and psychotherapy.* Springfield, IL: Charles C Thomas.
7. Rolling Stones. (1986) *Let it bleed.* (LP) New York: ABKCO Records.
8. Moon, B. (1992) *Essentials of art therapy training and practice.* Springfield, IL: Charles C Thomas.
9. Papini, G. (1969) *Existential psychology and psychiatry,* 9, n.2.
10. Hillman, J. (1989) *A blue fire.* New York: Harper & Row.
11. Simon, P. (1983) *Hearts and bones.* (LP) New York: Warner Brothers Records.
12. Berne, E. (1972) *What do you say after you say hello.* New York: Bantam Books.
13. *Webster's New World Dictionary. Third College Edition:* (1988) New York: Simon & Schuster.
14. Rice, T., Webber, A.L. (1970) *Jesus Christ Superstar* London: Leeds Music; New York.
15. Fromm, E. (1955) *The sane society.* New York: Fawcett World Library.
16. Jones, D. (1974) *Some assumptions about the therapeutic use of art.* Unpublished Paper.
17. Jones, D. (1983) An art therapist's personal record. *Journal of the American Art Therapy Association, Vol. 1* #1.
18. McNiff, S. (1992) *Art as medicine.* Boston: Shambala.
19. Allen, P. (1992) Artist in residence; an alternative to "clinification" for art therapists. *Journal of the American Art Therapy Association, Vol. 9,* Number 1.
20. Bly, R. (1990) *Iron John.* New York: Addison Wesley
21. Yalom, I. (1975) *Theory and practice of group psychotherapy.* New York: *Basic Books*
22. McNiff, S. (1989) Depth psychology of art. Springfield, IL: Charles C Thomas.
23. Moon, C. (1989) *Art as prayer.* Unpublished Paper
24. Goldschmidt, W. (1963) as quoted by D.A. Hamburg, Emotions in perspective of human evolution, in P. Knapp, ed., *Expressions of Emotions of Man.* New York: International Universities Press
25. Huestis, R., Ryland, C. (1990) Outcome after partial-hospital treatment of

severely disturbed adolescents. *International Journal of Partial Hospitalization,* Vol. 6, Number 2.

26. Gossett, J., Lewis, J., & Barnhard, F. (1983) *To find a way: the outcome of hospital treatment of disturbed adolescents.* New York: Brunner/Mazel.

27. Pirsig, R. (1974) *Zen and the art of motorcycle maintenance.* New York: Bantam Books.

28. Menninger, K. (1942) *Love against hate.* New York: Harcourt Brace.

29. Collins, J. (1972) My father. Who knows where the time goes. (LP) New York: Elektra Records.

30. Kopp, S. (1971) Guru: metaphors from a psychotherapist. Palo Alto: Science and Behavior Books

31. American Art Therapy Association. Code of Ethics

32. Bass, S. (1968) *Why man creates.* 16mm film/video. Designed, written and directed by Saul Bass. Santa Monica: Pyramid Films

INDEX